Healing
the
BROKEN
HEART

Healing the
BROKEN
HEART

SIN, ALIENATION and
the GIFT of GRACE

SUSAN L. NELSON

Chalice Press
St. Louis, Missouri

Cover Illustration: Bob Watkins
Art Director: Michael Domínguez

10 9 8 7 6 5 4 3 2 1   97 98 99 00 01 02

Library of Congress Cataloging—in—Publication Data
Nelson, Susan Louise.
   Healing the broken heart : sin, alienation, and the gift of grace /
   Susan Louise Nelson.
           p.   cm.
      Includes bibliographical references.
      ISBN 0-8272-1427-8
      1. Sin.   2. Alienation (Theology)   3. Forgiveness of sin.
   4. Grace (Theology)   I. Title.
   BT715.N43   1996   96-36859
   241'.3—dc21   CIP

Printed in the United States of America

Acknowledgments

I am a rock;
I am an island.
—Paul Simon

Of course, none of us is an island unto ourselves. Each of us is dependent upon the support and presence of others to be who we are. I'd like to thank many people who have encouraged me throughout this writing project.

First, I'd like to thank my community at Pittsburgh Theological Seminary: the Board for granting me sabbatical time; President C. S. Calian and Dean Richard Oman for making that time possible; the staff at Barbour Library for their energy and humor—particularly John Fry for his bibliographical assistance; several colleagues who read drafts of my work and provided feedback—George Kehm, Byron Jackson, John Mehl, and Sam Calian; the Faculty Development Committee who granted me funds to travel and network; the mailroom staff; my secretary Sheryl Gilliland for her help and good cheer; and the many students who thoughtfully responded to my early efforts to shape and present this material.

Several friends from the School of Theology at Claremont provided support and challenges: Marjorie Suchocki, ever a wonderful dialogue partner, also graciously shared her lovely home with me; Cathy Black provided her hot tub, many hours of conversation, and several key resources; Mary Elizabeth Moore offered, as always, gracious affirmation; the Center for Process Studies hosted me and coordinated my time in Claremont; Kathi Breazeale coordinated my visit and shared with me her insights as well as her bibliography; Jean and John Cobb provided hospitality and listening hearts—and

John continues, as he has for a long time, to support me and offer sage counsel.

I also want to thank several friends in Pittsburgh who offered greatly appreciated enthusiasm: Sara Penn-Strah read my draft with careful thought; Rebecca Ball, as student and friend, was a source of energy and good companionship; Ev Vogeley read each chapter as it was written and provided instant response and much-needed encouragement; Dave Lutz also read each chapter and always responded with his years of practice as a pastoral counselor, his kind and loving heart, and his experience as one who knows how to dance in alienation as well as how to heal. I am especially grateful to my family for being my family, for their love and support, and for allowing me to tell some of our story.

Finally I'd like to thank Chalice Press for publishing my work—and particularly David Polk, who received it with great enthusiasm and has guided it toward publication.

Susan L. Nelson

Contents

Introduction

S in has become a more acceptable topic of conversation than it was twenty years ago when Karl Menninger published *What Ever Became of Sin*.[1] We know and admit to ourselves now that people violate one another, that nations and ethnic groups are bound up in cycles of resentment and restitution, that structures of injustice persist and shape the way we know ourselves in this world, and that human beings are responsible for these situations and the behavior that created them.

We also now know—through the voices of theologians from the "underside"[2] of history—that in "doing theology," context and social location matter. We realize that all sin does not look alike, that oppressors and oppressed bring different perspectives to the dialogue about sin and brokenheartedness, and that race and gender are not insignificant.

In the past fifteen years our awareness of victimization has also expanded. We now acknowledge that incest happens, that alcoholism exists and affects whole family systems, that the amount and type of attention we give our children affects their abilities to function as whole human beings, and that systems of poverty, racism, and sexism affect not only how we relate to one another, but how we know and value ourselves.

To talk about sin in a complex and ambiguous world is not a simple matter. If Augustine once argued that human beings were born into a state of original sin and because of that cannot *not* sin, then our post-modern sense of life's relationality, vulnerability, and interconnection repeats to us that innocence is not a possibility— that our actions (or inactions) will have hurtful implications for someone caught in the same web of life of which we are a part.[3]

In this text, I want to focus on one particular aspect of our conversation about sin—that is, how the fact that human beings often experience "refusals" in our formative years (that damage us and shape the way in which we know and present ourselves to each other and the world, and the way in which we receive each other and the world back again, affects our talk about sin. The language of sin has at times been used to describe a sense that life (our lives and the world around us) is not the way it ought to be,[4] that we have individually and collectively fallen short of the mark, and that our alienation is a form of bondage from which we need rescue. But is the language of sin appropriate when the alienation and failure of which we speak are born not of rebellion or a desire to be god (as classical Christianity has defined sin), but out of what Rita Nakashima Brock has called a broken heart?[5] How does the fact that refusals and damage litter the pages of history (when we look at those pages with eyes attuned to see and appreciate the horror of this damage) and may even be the core from which some of us act in ways damaging to others and ourselves inform our theological conversation about sin? How can our talk of sin be sensitive to these distinctions?

In order to address these questions, this book is divided into three parts. Part I explores our understanding of the human condition and how that condition is the context for our sin. Chapter 1 looks at issues that will inform our conversation; chapter 2 explores the human condition; chapter 3 seeks to understand sin in the context of the previous chapters.

Part II—Sin and the Broken Heart: The Possibility of Being Refused—introduces the concept of "refusals" and "brokenheartedness." It looks at three dances of alienation born of brokenheartedness and asks in what way the language of sin is helpful and appropriate in understanding these dances. Chapter 4 looks at the Dance of Shame; chapter 5 explores the Dance of the Generations; and chapter 6 describes the situation of the Dance of Control—when the "dance" becomes a "march." Chapter 7 draws some conclusions about using the language of sin to speak about brokenheartedness.

Part III—Salvation: Healing Our Broken Hearts—argues that those who are brokenhearted need salvation not only from sin but from their brokenheartedness as well. Chapter 8 looks at healing; and the final chapter raises some questions about God that emerge in the context of brokenheartedness.

In writing about sin and brokenheartedness, there are three theologians in particular upon whose work I have built. The first is Edward Farley. Through his book *Good and Evil: Interpreting a Human Condition*,[6] Farley first made clear to me the contours of ambiguity and vulnerability that are implicit in the human condition as we know it. His description of the dimension of the interhuman—that realm of the in-between—has made possible my exploration into brokenheartedness and how it interfaces with human sin. Rita Nakashima Brock, in *Journeys by Heart*, has made the important point that sinful alienation and behavior may well be symptomatic of an underlying brokenheartedness. My work builds on hers to address how the language of sin is and is not appropriately applied to the brokenhearted. Finally, Marjorie Hewett Suchocki, in her book *Fall to Violence*,[7] has made the case that inherited behavior can be understood as both inherited (and therefore a "given") and yet sinful (and something for which we are responsible) in the context of a new possibility that turns inherited behavior from "given" to "a choice." She has helped me understand how sin language can be used to talk about brokenheartedness.

While I have drawn on the work of these theologians—as well as the work of many other thinkers whose contributions will be noted throughout the text—this work is drawn primarily from my own experience and that of those who have shared some of their stories with me. Because of this context, I do not make universal claims about the usefulness of my argument. But I do expect that it will contribute to the on going conversation about sin and human alienation.

And so, as Max of *Where the Wild Things Are* proclaims: "Let the rumpus begin!"[8]

---

[1] Karl Menninger, *What Ever Became of Sin?* (New York: Hawthorn Books, 1973).

[2] See Mary Potter Engel and Susan Brooks Thistlethwaite, eds., *Lift Every Voice* (San Francisco: Harper, 1990), for examples of the voices of people from the underside and for an argument for the importance of context in the theological project.

[3] See Kathleen Sands, *Escape from Paradise* (Minneapolis: Fortress Press, 1994), for an explication of this fall from innocence.

[4] See Cornelius Plantinga, *Not the Way It's Supposed to Be: A Breviary of Sin* (Grand Rapids, Michigan: Eerdmans, 1995).

[5] Rita Nakashima Brock, *Journeys by Heart* (New York: Crossroads, 1988).

[6] Edward Farley, *Good and Evil: Interpreting a Human Condition* (Minneapolis: Fortress Press, 1990).

[7] Marjorie Hewett Suchocki, *The Fall to Violence: Original Sin in Relational Theology* (New York: Continuum, 1994).

[8] Maurice Sendak, *Where the Wild Things Are* (San Francisco: Harper and Row, 1963).

Part I

T o be alive today is to live with pain. For some of us, our pain is the daily struggle to survive and to find a safe place to live. Others of us work to lift oppressive barriers that silence us and batter us into submission. For those unable to hope or to find one sustaining, ennobling relationship, a quiet, desolate loneliness defines the center of our existence, a center sometimes hidden by intense, aimless activity or hollow friendships. To live with our pain without some comprehension is to exist in the denial of pain or in the overwhelming, intractable presence of it. Both lead to despair.

Rita Nakashima Brock[1]

SIN
AND THE
HUMAN
CONDITION

Chapter 1

A Conversation

We are sinking deep in sin
    won't you come and pull us in,
With our attitudes toward sex
    we will all be nervous wrecks.
We are sinking deep in sin,
    whee-e-e-e.....
        —Message on stall in girls' bathroom, circa 1960

This is an invitation to a conversation about sin. But sin is not easy to talk about. For instance....

My husband and I spent a week at Ghost Ranch in Abiquiu, New Mexico, leading a seminar entitled "Sin, Shame, and Salvation." We were warned by those in charge of publicity that the word "sin" might not attract people to our class. We decided to use it anyway. But when we were asked by some ministers attending an interim ministry workshop held at the ranch during the same week what our class was about, we noticed that the word "sin" evoked strange giggles, smirks, and the comment, spoken through a rather lascivious grin, "We all know what that is about!" I wondered if, indeed, "we" did know what sin is about!...

My father died a few days after Christmas several years ago. On the following New Year's Eve, my siblings, our spouses, and our mother gathered in her living room to meet with the attending minister and do what perhaps most families do after the death of a loved one: tell stories about him. But, I noticed at the time, we were telling *careful* stories. We wanted to give the minister enough stories so that Dad's funeral would sound like it was about him—but, apparently, not enough stories so that the minister would see all the sides of our relationships with our father. I noticed that we censored stories about Dad's temper, the way at one time or another he had publicly shamed each of us—"dressing us down" before the scrutiny of our valued peers. We kept to ourselves our own ambivalence about his parenting, and the deep wounds that each of us had harbored and chosen not to share with one another. And as we talked and protected not only Dad but also ourselves from further public scrutiny, I was struck by my mother's comment that "If Dad were here, he wouldn't be here!"—pointing to my father's tendency to tuck himself away in front of a ball game or to become deeply intent upon a book rather than staying very long in family conversation. Suddenly I had the urge to go and find Dad—in the bedroom where he most likely would have been—and ask him to help me understand why he had behaved the way he had. I wanted to ask him whether at times he had lost his temper because the pain of life had gotten to be too much for him. (He had, after all, lost his own father when he was only six weeks old. He had weathered the storms of misfortune when my mother—at age 22—was stricken with polio. And he had suffered with her the resulting paralysis that had confined her to a wheelchair for the remainder of their life together.) I wanted to know whether he had isolated himself from the rest of the family because conversations had been too uncomfortable for him, too full of possible conflicts and hurt. Did his "lashings out" (as I called them) at his family reflect not some awful defect in us but the frustrations of his own wounded soul? And had he ever reflected about how they might have affected his family and wished to make amends but had not known how? Sadly, at the moment when I might have achieved a glimmer of intimacy with the man whose distance had so shaped my life, I knew that he was gone. I was struck at the moment by the tragic situation of having missed each other—at the awful fragility of life, that it could end before I was ready for it to end. And I pondered upon the damage that he, probably unintentionally, had wrought on each of his loved ones, and wondered how to hold together both truths: that he had hurt us (which I considered sin) and that he most probably had hurt those he loved out of his own pain and frustration (which was both awful and understandable)....

In the fall of 1995 my husband and I took a trip to Palestine and Israel. I felt in myself at the time of our departure a desire to focus on the "ancient stones" of the Holy Land and to avoid the mire of the Palestinian/Israeli conflict and the "living stones" that were crying out on both sides of the conflict for justice. The problem, I felt, was bigger than I was—so I tried to protect myself from their pain and my own powerlessness. But as our trip unfolded, as we left Galilee for the West Bank, I felt myself drawn to the plight of the Palestinians despite my inner commitment never to forget the horrors of the Holocaust for the Jewish people. I heard Palestinian stories of stolen land and water, torture, and ghettoization—some of them told by Christians whose lineage in the tradition was far more ancient than my own. I met young men who had thrown Molotov cocktails, and heard stories of Israeli soldiers who had amazed themselves with the brutality with which they responded to Molotov cocktails being thrown at them. I visited the Holocaust Museum in Jerusalem and remembered again the horrible atrocities the Jewish people have suffered. But I also noticed that some of those tales of horror could find echoes in the voices of the Palestinians I'd come to know. I realized through a little study that my own country's policies toward Israel implicated me in this land and its struggles. And I came to realize that no amount of protective distance—no "blessed ignorance" (which I lost forever, if I ever had it, on this trip)—would keep me innocent in this conflict....

A year ago, my son had a "falling out" with his good friend Rebecca. This alienation at first caused them both great anger and suffering. Yet, neither of them seemed to have the wherewithal or the inclination to seek reconciliation. They simply went their separate ways. This separation was neither dormant nor without a spiraling effect, however, for both of them shared their hurt feelings with their own circle of family and friends. Thus instead of two people being separated from one another, there was a network of alienation where those "caught in the middle" found it awkward to communicate with those on the "other side," and felt powerless to resolve the conflict. A year later—perhaps reflecting the serendipity of the holiday season—they happened to run into one another and were drawn into conversation. As a result of this encounter, they ended up renewing their friendship. When I asked my son how they had resolved their initial disagreement, he said they didn't even remember exactly what had caused their spiraling alienation in the first place. Glad for the reconciliation, I pondered both the healing and the damage....

In June of 1995 the *New York Times Magazine* featured an article about evil[2]—an article that explored situations of undeserved suffering and some of the ambiguous and messy murder cases that had captured the nation's attention in its recent past: the case of Susan Smith, who had been accused of murdering her two sons and was herself a victim of abuse, and that of the Menendez brothers who also claimed to be victims of their parents' abuse but who, in their killing spree, had stopped to reload (and, by implication, reflect). The author related what she believed to be the restlessness of the American people in the face of a growing number of "victim defense" strategies. The American public, she argued, is demanding that people be held accountable for their actions—insisting that victimhood cannot be enough of an answer to explain the horrible violence and murder and to exonerate the defendants of their responsibility. How, I wondered upon reading this article, can we hold both together—that people are both victims and perpetrators, that both conditions need to be confessed and healed? And can we end cycles of violation that murder innocent victims—or twist them into perpetrators (a twisting in which they might, in some way, be held complicit)?...

When I was a graduate student, I presented a paper for my women-in-theology group on the sin of hiding[3]—calling the sin of women not pride but a desire to hide. I did this knowing for myself that I and many of my friends suffered both from this sin of hiding and from the damaging practice in church each Sunday of confessing a sin of pride and self-assertion that was not our own. My hope (and experience) was that a call to confess the right sin might be healing. My paper, however, was met with both excitement (as some could feel the possibility of liberation in the message) and anger— as some felt that in naming women's hiding as sinful I was in effect blaming the victims, thereby only adding to the guilt women in a patriarchal society already carried. I was caught between my awareness that hiding is often a survival tactic for women in such a society and is a way of being in the world taught to women before we may be conscious of the damage it creates (or before we have help in imagining other ways of being), and my conviction that women are complicit to varying degrees in our own hiddenness and that naming that complicity is a step toward claiming new possibilities for ourselves....

Conversation about sin is not easy. It means facing the discomfort the word *sin* arouses. It means tackling the differences between the alienations and grief that life brings us simply because of our limitations of time and space, and the way in which we (even unintentionally) "violate the image of God in others and ourselves."[4] It means asking questions about our responsibility for violation of another when such violation was never our initial intent. It means acknowledging that some people are victims of others' abuse and that such abuse is important in understanding why those same people can then inflict violence upon others. It is to raise the question of complicity and responsibility in the face of great social pressures to hide one's possibilities and responsibilities. It is to realize that injustices are carried for generations, wounding the souls of those born into it—and that conflictual situations are often more complex than a simplistic righteous vs. sinner scenario would suggest.

Conversation about sin is further complicated by our contemporary sensibility that the language of sin can be used as a form of social control.[5] Feminist texts have clearly argued that blaming Eve for sin (as well as conflating sexuality with sin and blaming women for that as well) has functioned as a strategy for naming all women as "other"—second-class citizens[6]—or that the church has used the doctrine of sin to create inside the laity a watchful eye that freely dispenses guilt and shame and functions to keep people "in line."[7] Moreover, as I will argue, the word *sin*, used to name feelings of guilt resulting from being the victim of another's sin, can effectively keep victims from seeing and being healed of their wounds.

We also now know, as mentioned in the Introduction, that social location matters, that the sins of the oppressors (perhaps pride and domination) are not the same as the sins of the oppressed (complicity and hiding), that "sin language" written uncritically from the perspective of those with power and directed at those with much less power is destructive—and that the word "sin" itself may not even be appropriate to express the alienation experienced by those who are victims.[8] Further, many of us can be both the oppressor and the oppressed.

Despite these questions and constraints, I believe a contemporary conversation about sin is possible. But, out of respect for the questions raised above, certain observations are in order about how this conversation is possible .

First, while respecting the classical Augustinian intuition that sin is original—larger than the individual; a state of bondage that reflects a divided self—this conversation will present different presuppositions about the human condition than those that have grounded the Augustinian view. We will look at the suffering, conflicts, and ambiguities of the human situation as structured into life as we have it and not as the result of a primal fall (while also acknowledging that sin greatly amplifies the suffering, conflict, and ambiguities that are already given to life as we know it). This will lead us to new conclusions about sin that affirm the Augustinian tradition's description of the bondage of human beings to sin but offer a different understanding of the source of that bondage and a different interpretation of how that bondage works.

Second, evil and suffering are assumed to be real, and sin language will not be used to protect us from seeing evil and suffering. Someone once suggested to me that there would be no "problem of bad things happening to good people"[9] if we believed that people are not good. The doctrine of original sin has been used by the tradition in this way to explain away the death of small (and therefore presumably innocent) children. Supposedly, this protects God from being charged with the injustice of those deaths. It may also reflect, as Elaine Pagels has suggested, a human tendency to choose to be guilty of sin rather than acknowledge that we are helpless to fully protect ourselves and those we love in a world where suffering and evil happen. She asks:

> What are we to make, I wonder, of this peculiar preference for guilt? Augustine would, I suspect, take it as evidence that human nature itself is "diseased," or, in contemporary terms, neurotic. I would suggest, instead, that such guilt, however painful, offers reassurance that such events do not occur at random but follow specific laws of causation; and that their causes, or a significant part of them, lie in the moral sphere, and so within human control.[10]

Some have argued that this view of sin actually turns God into a monster who punishes all humanity because of the fault of the two original human beings.[11] Original sin language, if it is to be useful to contemporary people, cannot protect us or God in this way.

Third, life is tragic. By tragic I do not mean that it is never happy, or that there are no happy endings. By tragic I mean—as alluded to earlier—that life is structured with possibilities and limits, vitalities and vulnerabilities, ambiguities, harmonies and conflicts. This is the context out of which great adventure, beauty, joy and satisfaction can emerge. It is also a context laced with insecurities, suffering, and anxiety. Here, I agree with those theologians of the Kierkegaardian strain of the Christian tradition who see the human situation as the context—the precondition—out of which our sin emerges. This means that not all conflict and suffering are the result of sin. It also means that sin is something for which we are responsible, even though it may be a responsibility we discover and confess about ourselves only at a later time because we originally acted not with the intent to sin, but with the more socially acceptable intent of making ourselves more secure. This view of sin and the human condition will be more fully developed in the next two chapters of this section.

Fourth, when we speak of sin, we are speaking of more than individual acts of sin. There is a certain pattern to sin in our lives. It accumulates, sediments, and shapes us, becoming a part of us. It has an influence. Thus, I agree with liberation theologians who find sin in our systems and institutions of oppression. I also find resonance, however, with those who speak of sin as alienation or estrangement from God, self, and others that is not only between persons but within the individual. However, while affirming that alienations from God, self and others are both real and paralyzing, I question whether all paralyzing alienations are best named sin.[12] (I will discuss this point in Section II.)

Fifth, we live in a relational universe—and we ourselves are constructed in a relational fashion. This means that relationships constitute who we are—they are not "accidental" to our sovereign selfhood. We construct ourselves out of and in the midst of our relationships and they matter. This also means that human beings are vulnerable and dependent. Thus, when we talk about sin, we do so in the context of relationships that matter, and in the very real face of dependencies and interdependencies that leave us vulnerable to wounding. This wounding needs to be a significant piece of our reflection on sin.

Sixth, we live in a post-modern world—well aware of the constructed nature of all our meanings, even of our very selfhood. If sin is *selfhood and relationships constructed in an alienating way* (which I will argue that it is), we must be clear how this form of self- and relationship-construction differs from any form of self- or socially constructed reality (assuming both that all constructed reality is somehow alien—constructed in compromise with the society and not fully reflective of the best possibility of one's being). While none of us can be anything other than constructed, some constructions are more alienating that others. We will explore some constructions of self born of alienation, assuming that the selves constructed in healing and forgiveness are more inclusive of all the pieces of our selves and therefore are less alienating than other constructions of self.

Finally, as noted in the Introduction, our modern sensibility awakens us to the complexity of our world, where systems and lives are so interwoven that it is impossible not to be mired in some way in the sufferings of others. This was reflected in my experience of the Palestinian/Israeli conflict. But it is also reflected in the fact that when I buy bananas for thirty-nine cents a pound, I am participating in an unjust system that pays workers less than a living wage. This means on the one hand that it is no longer possible to be innocent of others' suffering, and on the other that postures of innocence (for instance, seeking to be good so that others will love us) can mire us more deeply in alienating systems and dances that turn the spontaneous mystery that is the dance of life into compulsive, despairing, and controlling dances that squeeze the joy and mystery out of the lives we are given.

My daughter Kathryn was diagnosed with a brain tumor when she was thirteen years old. Luckily for us, we live in a city with a surgeon who was expert in just the surgery she needed. Within one week after her diagnosis, she was on the operating table. Her surgery was successful. (And the tumor was benign—although how anyone can call a brain tumor benign is beyond me.) Her recovery has been slow, but steady and successful as well.

When Kathryn came home from the hospital, we gave her a new kitty to keep her company during her recovery. I suppose in some way I wanted to distract her from the horror she had just faced and weathered. Perhaps I also wanted to protect myself from the reality that her life had been threatened. Sadly, Kathryn's kitty did not thrive as well as she did. Within a few months, it had developed a congenital disease of the spine that we were told would be fatal. The night before we took "Rumpy" (for Rumpelstiltskin,) to the veterinarian to be "put to sleep," Kathryn looked at me with eyes full of tears and said, "It's okay, Mom. It was worth it."

That sentence captured for me several truths about life: the truth that life hurts; the truth that we often want to protect ourselves from such hurt by avoiding life (and the relationships that can be so life-sustaining and can enhance our experience of life's fragility); the reality that this avoiding of life might be both understandable and sinful; and the experience that in the courage to risk life and all it might bring, we can find that life still has the promise of giving us more than it takes.[13] This is the context in which our lives are given us. It is the context in which we will begin to talk about sin.

---

[1] Rita Nakashima Brock, *Journeys by Heart*, p. 1.

[2] Ron Rosenbaum, "Staring into the Heart of the Heart of Darkness," *The New York Times Magazine*, June 4, 1995, pp. 36–45, 50, 58–61, 72.

[3] Susan Nelson Dunfee, "The Sin of Hiding: A Feminist Critique of Reinhold Niebuhr's Account of the Sin of Pride," *Soundings*, Vol. LXV, No. 3, Fall 1982, pp. 316–327. This paper captured many of the points made earlier by Valerie Saiving and Judith Plaskow.

[4] This line is taken from the confession of sin embedded in the "Brief Statement of Faith" of the Presbyterian Church (USA).

[5] Michel Foucault has argued that social discourse—and the arrangement of knowledge in a society—are modes of social control. For a study of the work of Foucault, see David R. Shumway, *Michel Foucault* (Charlottesville: University of Virginia Press, 1989).

[6] Mary Daly, *Beyond God the Father* (Boston: Beacon Press, 1973).

[7] See Elizabeth A. Clark's article, "Sex, Shame, and Rhetoric: En-Gendering Early Christian Ethics," *JAAR*, Summer 1991, Vol. LIX, No. 2, pp. 221–246, for an exploration of the use of shame in the preaching of the patristic fathers.

[8] This is the insight of *Minjung* theologians—among others. See Andrew Sung Park, *The Wounded Heart of God*. (Nashville: Abingdon Press, 1993).

[9] Although the awareness of this problem is older than Job, this particular formulation echoes the title of Rabbi Harold Kushner's book *When Bad Things Happen to Good People*. (New York: Avon, 1981).

[10] Elaine Pagels, *Adam, Eve and the Serpent* (New York: Random House, 1988).

[11] See Elizabeth A. Clark's article on baptism, "From Originism to Pelagianism: Elusive Issues in an Ancient Debate," in *The Princeton Seminary Bulletin*, n.s.12, No. 3, 1991, pp. 283–303, to see how both sides of this argument could present themselves as protecting God from the charge of being a monster.

[12] Theologians have often made the distinction between sins (acts of violations against others, ourselves, our world) and Sin (a state or condition of alienation or bondage). When I speak of sin, I link the two phenomena together. This will become clearer in chapter 3.

[13] Of course, for many people, life does take more than it gives. The fact that there are victims of unjust systems who never have the same opportunities for life as others proves this point. My point here is only that the vulnerability of life in itself speaks not only of the risk of hurt and disappointment but also of the pleasures of genuine acceptance, connection, and community.

Chapter 2

That's Life

Many's the time I've been mistaken
*   and many times confused*
Yes, and I've often felt forsaken
*   and certainly misused...*

And I don't know a soul who's not been battered
*   I don't have a friend who feels at ease*
I don't know a dream that's not been shattered
*   or driven to its knees*

But it's all right, it's all right
*   For we've lived so well so long*
Still, when I think of the road we're traveling on
I wonder what's gone wrong.
*   I can't help it, I wonder what's gone wrong.*
                    —"An American Tune," Paul Simon

In the film *My Life* actor Michael Keaton assumes the role of Bob Jones—a man who has discovered in early middle age that he has terminal cancer. Jones (originally named Bobby Ivanovich) was born in a Midwestern city and raised by immigrant parents. His father was by some standards hardworking; by Bob's standards he was never home. Jones changed his name and escaped his family and perhaps all the messiness of life that it represented to him. He moved to California where he established himself as a self-made, hard-driving public relations man very much in control of his life but also very hard to live with. At the peak of his career Bob learns, and tries to avoid the fact, that he has only months to live. The movie shows how Jones—his dream "driven to its knees"—faces his fears and anger about life, uncovers his grief that life didn't give him more than it did, and is able to see, finally, how much he has been given. ("But, it's all right, it's all right.") By preparing a video for the son his wife is carrying (and eventually births) and whom he fears he will never know, Jones creates the opportunity to tell his son about himself and to share with his son all the lessons about life he will never have a chance to teach him in person. This act of reconstructing his life before the video camera transforms Jones's experience of his life from "that's life" (said with irony and resistance) to "my life"—one filled with wisdom, love, reconciliation, acceptance, and peace. The beauty of the film is not only that Jones models for viewers a hope that one can know life with all its disappointments and suffering and still find adventure and joy, but that it achieves this goal without denying the vulnerabilities, ambiguities, and fears that constitute of life as we know it.

In order to converse about sin, we need first to talk about "life," the human condition, for life is the crucible in which sin is formed. Unlike Adam and Eve, the archetypal humans for much of the Christian tradition, you and I were not created from the dust of the earth.[1] Nor were we like that first creature created alone without human community, nor were we placed in an idyllic garden with the ready companionship of our Creator. Rather, we were given not just "life" but "a life," complete with all the trappings as we know them. We were conceived in the coming together of two human persons (hopefully in an act of love), birthed through the blood and pain of a woman, caught (if we were fortunate) by welcoming hands, marveled at by a waiting community, and (again, hopefully) nurtured, protected, and taught as we were introduced into the journey of life. Our lives have a history, a particular community, a set of challenges, a range of relationships, an inheritance of skills, stories, inhibitions, and expectations, an array of possibilities beyond what any of us could manage in a lifetime—and all of these are significant as we begin our conversation about life and about sin.

The life we have been given is far from easy.[2] It is fraught with tensions and anxieties, with opportunities and losses, with confusion and mastery, with possibilities and limits, with community and isolation, with tenderness and with the stark reality of death. It is haunted by parental expectations, by losses remembered or long buried, by our own perhaps forgotten hopes and fears of disappointment. All of these pull and tear at us and form the context out of which we each construct a life. In presenting life in this way, I am not saying that the world is evil, but that suffering, ambiguity, and conflict are pieces of the world as constructed. Nor am I suggesting that the stresses and strains should be construed as the result of human sin—although I would agree that sin adds a deeper dimension of suffering and conflict to the conflict and ambiguity that are already there. Challenge and exhilaration, disappointment and limitations—and the joy and suffering they entail—are pieces of life. Let me elaborate.[3]

To be human (to be any creature, for that matter!) is to be born into a world over which we have little control. Those of us in the first world—perhaps like the self-made Bob Jones—are able to have control over much of our lives. We can decide where to live, whom to marry, how many children to have, what kind of diet to follow. As a nation, we have control over which lands will be developed, and which ones left as natural reserves, which species will be protected, which river basins will be claimed for farmland. But then there is a flood, or the discovery of an ecological system unredeemedly disrupted far beyond our intentions, or our favorite baseball team fails to win the playoffs even though we loyally attend each game, or a sister-in-law forms an unfavorable perception of me perhaps because I am a minister and she hates ministers and doesn't even bother to get to know me and see that *I* am different, or our child's kitten dies, and we confront the reality of the limit of our control. Despite our best efforts to fix the broken toy, to express ourselves carefully so that people will understand what we really mean, we are limited, people misconstrue our motives all the time, and that is hard. When my oldest daughter was tiny and some part of her life came apart, I tried very hard to fix it so that she would know that the world was not scary and overwhelming; when my youngest daughter faced a similar tragedy, on my best days I sat and cried with her. Life *is* scary and overwhelming and we have to find our ways in the midst of it.

We also live in a world that is structured with ambiguity and conflict, where our best efforts often do not lead to the results we have anticipated, where our deeply held loyalties conflict with each other, where we have to make hard choices in the awareness that everyone cannot win. When my sister was ten years old, she planned a birthday party. She invited seven other little girls to her party—the total being governed by the number of "special" plates, napkins, and party hats that came in the manufacturer's party package: eight. The day of my sister's party, a new girl enrolled in her class and my sister—being the generous, gregarious person she has always been—invited her new friend to her party. And then her best and happiest intentions boomeranged on her—for an extra person meant that my sister would have to give up her "special" party plate and hat and napkin for her new friend. This was more than my sister could bear, and she spent much of her party—at least to my memory—in her bedroom. Things just didn't go as planned—she got sideswiped. And even though this example might seem trivial to an adult (surely she could have been coaxed into accepting a different kind of plate as being even more special since she was "the birthday girl"), it's not so different from the times when we have put all our best energies into planning an event, studying for a test, running for elected office, only to have our best efforts misconstrued or unrewarded in the manner we justifiably anticipated.

Then again, we know how it feels to be torn apart when just causes conflict. A single father on a very limited income wants to protect his children from worry about the family finances but also is committed to living carefully within their budget. He must construct a careful balancing act to do justice to both of his loyalties. A middle-aged woman is offered the opportunity of her professional life, a position with more responsibility and the possibility for making a difference in her field. However, to accept the opportunity, she will have to uproot her family from the house they have built over the years into a home, from the friends they need in order to be who they are, from the schools with all the security they offer and the challenges they present—especially to her teenagers, who very definitely do not want to move in the middle of their high school years. Or, a nation has to decide whether to increase spending on national defense or education, on medical research for mechanical hearts, or funding for "universal" basic health care. An African-American woman feels the compexity of herself and her world as situations demand that she name either the struggle against sexism or the movement to resist racism (and not both) as her primary loyalty.

Life confronts us with ambiguities and conflicts and hard choices, many of which have within them the possibilities for even more exciting choices. (Could we restructure our spending so that we didn't need to choose between funding research for AIDS *or* for breast cancer?) These choices can be awful (Which limited few shall benefit from our limited resources?), or exhilarating (Shall I travel to Europe this summer, or be a volunteer in mission at a school in Alaska?), or both. Often they are made in maddening ignorance. (How much do I really know about what is going to happen between now and next summer? Can I really know what a summer teaching in Alaska will be like? How will my choices affect the rest of my family? How can we know before they happen?) The point is that they add more intensity and stress into the pot.

We also live in a world where there is not only conflict and possibility, but where conflict and possibility and hope and joy (as well as death and suffering) entail loss. A new job means the loss of an old way of being and knowing. We "come of age" and our status changes—we gain the possibilities and responsibilities of adulthood, but sometimes we miss the privilege of being children. We marry and our relationships with our lover-turned-spouse and with our friends change. We have children and marvel as they grow and develop new skills; and then, one day, we find ourselves crying because our tall, handsome sons of whom we are so proud are no longer the endearing three-year-old little boys who used to whisper sweetly and intimately in our ears. We move, and find that we have lost not only neighborhoods and familiar places, but pieces of ourselves. My adolescent son once told me, when he was considering coming with me for a sabbatical year, that he was afraid of moving to a new place because it would feel like being "born again."

Like C.S. Lewis, as he is portrayed in the film *Shadowlands*, we are confronted with the reality that to love is to run the risk of losing (really, the actuality of losing), but that it is precisely this fragility that makes love so amazing and beautiful and surprisingly joyful. It is also what can make us feel so vulnerable in our loving and heighten our sense of worry. (On a different tack, a friend pointed out to me during the annual Cherry Blossom Festival in Washington, D.C., that people never alter their lives to go and see artificial flower arrangements. What draws us to the Tidal Basin to marvel at the beauty of the blossoms is precisely the fact that they come and go so quickly.)

This anxiety of living is further heightened because it appears that this is also a world in which bad things do happen to good people. Planes do crash, taking with them people who were in the prime of their lives. Righteous behavior does not guarantee one's well-being, and even diligent parents can have children with cancer. In the film *Safe Passages* a young man—who has a natural gift for running and has become a star of sorts—agonizes over the possibility that his brother has been killed in a military action. If only, he says, he had not beaten his brother at track, his brother wouldn't have quit the track team, and he wouldn't have started hanging out with a bunch of guys who then dropped out of school, and he wouldn't have joined the Marines and been sent to the Persian Gulf for the military action in which he was killed. If only he had lost the race, his brother wouldn't have died. And the young man's mother, who has agonized over her own inability to protect each of her sons from all dangers, turns to him (and to herself) and says: "Being a less than excellent runner will not make your brother safe!" His logic had been flawless; one thing did lead to another. But his brother's death or safety was still out of his control.

Not only is our *world* structured in a way that pulls and tears at us, drawing us off our centers, but our very being is structured with tensions and vulnerabilities that are the source of great richness— but which also threaten our very sense of well being. For example, consider these pieces of what it means to be human.

To be human is to be born as helpless and dependent children. We need others to catch us, hold us, mirror us, help us to know who we are and what we feel. We are dependent on others to protect us and help us grow into strong adults. We even build ourselves out of our relationships; our earliest important relationships provide a pattern for all our later relationships and are where we learn how to trust others, our world, ourselves, and the source and mystery of life. This means that our lives from the very start are vulnerable, for disappointments, mistakes, failures inevitably happen. Even the most attentive of fathers will one day get caught in traffic and be late to pick up his child. Even the most loving of mothers will come home tired and grouchy one day, unable for a while to give her husband and children what they need from her. This is not to suggest that she shouldn't be depleted—depletion is a fact of life—only that our needs and those of others will from time to time conflict. The life we are given is built of relational bridges that are intrinsic to who we are. Bridges break but can also be repaired. The rhythm of breaking and repairing is the pulse of life and becomes both the ground of hope (as we learn that broken bridges are not the final word) and the source of anxiety (as some bridges are not repaired— as some injuries come before we can tolerate them).

The vulnerabilities of our relational existence do not end with our childhood. To be human is to have what Emmanuel Levinas calls "face," and to desire "face-to-face" relations.[4] Each of us has a vulnerable, living, loving, needy self/face that we protect against the comings and goings of daily life. (This makes sense; it takes time and presence to see a face. Sadly, much of life doesn't offer this luxury.) But, this face needs to be seen, much like the "velveteen rabbit"[5] needed to be loved to be real. This face also needs others to see, to love, to feel compassion for and respond to. We desire to love and to be loved—to look with delight upon another and to have them look with equal delight upon us—and we are less ourselves when we fail to love. I pass a homeless man on the streets of Pittsburgh each week and I look away, unsure of what to do. My daughter reaches into her pocket, pulls out her allowance—a mere coin—and puts it in his cup. She has seen and responded to the man's face, whereas I have avoided it—and both he and I are less human because of it.[6]

But along with relationships of "face" comes the possibility of suffering. After all, one's face could be ignored or rejected by another; when one loves, one suffers with the loved one's pain; when one loves and disappoints the other, one suffers both the pain of disappointment in oneself and the pain one has caused the other. To risk face-to-face relation, then, is to know the possibility of great intimacy and great suffering; to fail to risk is to know depletion. Either way, to have a face is to know vulnerability.

To be human is also to be dependent upon human community to give us structures that support our living. We are dependent upon our societies for language and norms that help us to function successfully within our community. But the same society can also limit us. The norms it may give us may help us to function within the society but may thwart us from fully expressing ourselves. Norms of maleness and femaleness, for example, may at one time have been helpful norms for the survival of the human community. But those same norms can be the source of great suffering when men and women are not allowed to develop as fully as they could because of them. Similarly, racist norms have allowed some to thrive at the expense of others. Names we are given in childhood—"helpful," "dependable," "responsible"—that are at first affirming can become prisons as we later need to let go of a sense of responsibility that is larger than we could possibly be. Societies grant us support, and we tussle with them to find room for our own voices. The challenging of norms, finding the courage to speak in one's own voice (let alone knowing that one has a unique voice and has learned to recognize it), all put us in tension with the societies that shape us. A creative tension, perhaps, but still a tension.

To be human is to need the communities that hold us and give us life, and also to have the desire to be subjects "in our own right." It is to learn a dance between being held and venturing out to explore the world and find what it has to offer each of us in our own particularity.[7] It is to struggle with issues of care for others, for the communities that are essential to who we are, and care for ourselves—for our own expression and well-being. It is to realize that those who love us are also unique centers of being with their own perspectives that are not ours, with needs and desires that might conflict with our own. To discover the "otherness" of the ones we love is both bad news (we are not the center of the world after all; the ones who love us may also love others—may not always be there when we need them; our needs and theirs may and do conflict; we may not always get the affirmation we need) and good news (I am not all there is—there is another "face," a new mystery, to meet me, a different possibility for human community).[8]

This dance of self and other is further complicated by the layers of relationality that can distort one another. When my daughter was in college and very much in love with a naval midshipman, the two of us went to see the film *Born on the Fourth of July*. The film rehearsed all the issues of the Vietnam war years for me—and since that had been a time in my life when I had not yet developed my own "voice," I took advantage of our conversation after viewing the film to explain to my daughter how I felt about that war. My daughter had a different opinion, but so intent was I on finally expressing myself on this issue that I completely failed to listen to her well-thought-out views. In speaking loudly in my own voice (hearing inside my head, perhaps, the old context of my own student days)—striving for the "self" side of my dance between self and other—I failed to honor her newly found voice (thereby ironically replicating the silencing I had experienced in my student years). It was only when I realized that I was in fact operating on two levels of the dance of self and other (an older one, and the level between my daughter and myself where I had a different responsibility) that I was able to hear my daughter, apologize to her, and mend the bridge between us.

Sometimes the tension of the dance between self and the community of others is not only the tension of "leaving home" for the first time; sometimes it is also the ongoing dance of holding those we have covenanted to love while also seeking our own selfhood. A young mother of three—supremely gifted as a thinker and teacher, deeply committed to her children—fights an internal battle each morning as she prepares for work, feeling the need to justify her desire to both teach and mother. A naval officer struggles with his conflicting desires to advance in the Navy, which means regular six-month periods out at sea and away from home, and to be home to enjoy his young son's growing up (something he particularly values since his own father did not have this opportunity). A couple nearing retirement age consider selling the old family home (which has been the favored gathering place for all their children and grandchildren) and moving across the country to a retirement village in the Southwest. If they move, they will be able to remain self-sufficient and enjoy their independence for a longer period of time than if they remain in their large, three-storied home in the cold Northeast. Yet, if they move, they will not be as accessible to the family and friends that they value as well. To be individuals, with our own concerns and centers of being; to be in and value our communities that give us life and evoke in us a care for others that is also part of who we are—these are the various dances of intimacy. Exciting, even exhilarating, but not easy.

In addition, to be human is both to know the joys and frustration of being physical, embodied beings and also to experience the possibility of knowing ourselves as "having" bodies—of knowing ourselves as somehow not identical with our bodies.[9] Apart from the way in which our culture distorts embodied existence and lures us into a critical consciousness of our constructed body image, our bodies are a source of delight and frustration. They grant us pleasure; they ground us to this earth and its nurture in the rhythms that are endemic to our being.[10] As embodied beings, we have needs and desires that are basic to our survival. We need food, shelter, protective clothing, water, the warm touch of another, times of rest, periods of rigorous activity, solitude, genital sexual intimacy, bodily organs that function well and cooperate with one another, continuity, novelty, sunshine, shadows and shade, time and places to remember our connection with the natural world, music, beauty, dance. When we can experience these things, we know enjoyment and satisfaction. And when they are not available for us, we suffer frustration and even pain. Our basic needs are complexified as they become interwoven or conflict with one another. Our desire for touch, for example, can be confused with the desire for genital sexual expression. Our need for a regular pattern to our days (so that we don't have always to think about what comes next) can conflict with an urge for novelty. The desire for beauty can be frustrated because beauty fades (try to hold on to a sunset, for example), or the beauty that we have in our hands falls short of the desire that echoes in our hearts. (Of course, this could also be a goad to keep on looking and creating until you "find your dream.") Embodied life is full of possibilities for joy and frustration.

Embodied life also confronts us with our finitude. To be human is to be subject to limitations. We are all, to some degree, objects of destiny. We did not choose our genetic code; nor did we decide who our parents were to be or the extended families into which we would be born. We are dependent on these others—and this is both the source of great richness and of limitation—for we can form ourselves only out of the "stuff" that is at hand. Even our own personal histories exercise a power over which we have little conscious control.

We are subject to time—there are only so many hours in a day, days in a lifetime—and we are forced to decide how we shall use it. The choosing, and the fact that we have to choose, conspire to amplify our awareness of our limited time and perhaps even pressure us to make the most of what we have. And this creates more anxiety, since none of us knows exactly how much time we have. Exactly when is middle age? We can know that only when we get to the end.

And that end is also our limitation. Our embodied existence is one that finally culminates in death. Our bodies age and wear out, we don't look like ourselves anymore, and we find it harder to find the right "repair cream" that will restore us to vestiges of our youth.

We can celebrate the growth and increasing mastery of our children, at the same time remembering our own moments of such mastery and wondering to ourselves how time has gone so fast. (How is it possible that we are now the parents when we still feel like the kids?) We can experience our bodies as betraying us. Cal was a friend I had in California. I knew him only as a bent-over old man, tied to his oxygen tanks wherever he went. Cal had retired to California after years of work on the mission field. Unfortunately, it wasn't until his funeral that I learned that Cal had been a tall man (I'd never seen him standing upright), and that in his youth he had been a star tennis player. He had told the visiting pastor days before he died that inside he still felt like the same young man he had been on the tennis court. It had been so hard for him to accept his increasing disability. It felt to him like a betrayal. To be human is to be embodied, to know great joy, to suffer frustrations and aging, to die, and to be aware that all of this is happening. It is not only the aging and the injuries and the promise of death that add to our suffering, it is also our awareness of it all.

Despite the "facticity" of what is given us as life (be that the gene pool or the location of our birth), despite the real limitations that are always lurking on the edges of our consciousness, to be human is also to know a certain measure of freedom. This is reflected in our awareness of our limits, and in our search for beauty. It is echoed in our desire for something more, and in the ability to imagine what that something more might be. It is the grounds for our search for meaning—our insistence that life make sense and that it make a sense that we can understand. It is expressed in both our awareness and our disappointment that our systems of meaning won't work any longer. It is even the root of our terror that we might fail or die.

We are created with the possibility that we can be more than what we started out with. We can outgrow the nicknames our families (perhaps not so helpfully) gave us. For instance, I had a friend named Michael who once offered to fix my iron. As he sat at my kitchen table, my iron in pieces, his sister walked into the room and said: "What's he doing? Don't you know that he is 'Michael-who-takes-things-apart-and-can't-put-them-back-together-again'?" I had no idea that had been the nickname his family had given him, but he managed to fix my iron anyway—earning a new name in my book!

If we can't change those names, at least we can tell our families to stop using them. (As my sister once said, "I don't want to hear any more stories of the things I did when I was a kid. I was a kid then, for heaven's sake! Get to know me now!!") We can survive terrible catastrophes and even learn new things in their midst. I had been divorced for only a year when a good friend invited me to a Christmas party at her home. Thrilled to get an invitation (this was my first real party since my divorce), I arrived at the party full of hope but still feeling very fragile and wounded. When I saw and felt how happy and excited the other guests at the party were and how enthusiastically they greeted one another (with an enthusiasm I had yet to recover in myself), I retreated to the kitchen feeling lonely and totally unable to participate. After an hour of doing whatever I could to keep myself in the kitchen, I finally turned to my hostess, thanked her for the invitation, and told her that it was too much for me, that I had to leave. She hugged me and whispered in my ear, "That's fine. But I just want you to know that everyone here at this party has been where you are now at some time in his or her life." I looked at her to confirm the truth of what she had spoken. After a moment of thought, I slipped quietly into a chair by the Christmas tree to watch with a new curiosity the interplay of the party—learning how people who also had suffered divorce and isolation could live and enjoy life again. My friend's whisper in my ear was my Christmas present that year. It was a present of hope, which I in my own freedom and creativity (no matter how fragile I was at the moment) was able to latch onto.

Freedom, of course, isn't easy. It wasn't easy for me to stay at that party. It isn't always easy to dream a new dream and make it into an actuality. And when we do, life being what it is, it often means not only the joy of the adventure, but the reality of leaving behind the old (or relating to it in a new way), or the scariness of venturing into what we do not know for sure. Students at seminary do this every year. They perhaps sell their homes, pack up their families, move to a new city, enroll their children in inner city schools, face the shock of diversity, and discover that seminary means studying subjects that never occurred to them. Or they come alone, leaving well-established networks of friends, feeling scared but also excited about the new venture on their own. They are hesitant to make new friends—or perhaps are a little too gregarious. They are excited to learn, but intimidated by a whole new vocabulary. Some days they get it right; some days they return home mortified. And through it all, they ponder (if they don't outright worry): "Am I in the right place? Is this God's will in my life? What if I fail? What next?" To be free is a wonderful gift of our humanity, but it is not easy.

So, "that's life." Some days it's wonderful; some days it's agony. Most days it's a mixture of the two. It is a wonderful gift, a possibility full of beauty and pain and vulnerability. When I was a teenager I read the line in the Gospels, "The Son of Man has nowhere to lay his head" (Matthew 8:20) and finished it by adding "because there was no place comfortable for him." What I thought that day was that life was not easy, that there were no easy answers to what I would or should do with my life (not even in the Bible!), only lots of opportunities to make life my own. I felt that as neither good nor bad; it just was—and it was all right (as Paul Simon sings).

A life full of opportunities, possibilities, and conflicts, a life that is both limited and free, a life with feelings we do not always have the ability to express and that are not always heard when we do manage to express them,[11] a life full of desires that by definition cannot all be met, a life that is at heart relational and gifted with the consciousness that all of this, if true, is also a life that is vulnerable and less than secure. Most of us are blessed with anchors throughout our life. We have hometowns, jobs, loved ones, favorite places and songs and foods, precious memories, good health—all of which help us to secure ourselves, to know who we are. We can make homes, build communities, and construct meaning in our lives (reaching at times for a meaning that is larger than we are). But all our lives are vulnerable: our anchors can slip, our parents can die, we can lose jobs, radio stations can stop playing our favorite tunes, our backs can simply slip a disc, leaving us disabled and in great pain, we can contemplate an open (and promising or threatening?) future, we can watch our old meaning systems dissolve before our eyes, we can face overwhelming systems of injustice that deny us the full possibility of life, and we can anticipate death. We can know in ourselves a desire for a meaning that will not—in the tension and insecurity that life gives us—dissolve, a beauty that will not wither or fade, a love that will not let us go. This is the life we are given; this is the context in which we become selves; these are the stresses and strains that pull and tear us in many directions, amplifying our need to be secure; and this is the crucible in which our sin is formed and passed on from one to the other and to the next other along the way.

---

[1]Scientists now tell us that in our interrelated universe we *are* in fact created from the dust of the universe. In this rendition, the very "stuff" of dust is the reality of our connectedness.

[2] This was Søren Kierkegaard's initial insight and I am indebted to him. See *The Concept of Anxiety* (Princeton: Princeton University Press, 1980).

[3] This chapter is informed by the work of Edward Farley, particularly his book *Good and Evil*, where he outlines the way the human condition is structured in ambiguity, vulnerability, and conflict. I agree with Farley—as opposed to the classical Augustinian tradition that these pulls and tears of life are part of life's structure and are the precondition of sin. For a phenomenological approach to the ambiguity, conflict, challenge, freedom, relationality, and suffering of the human condition, see *Good and Evil*, Part I.

⁴See Farley's *Good and Evil*, p. 39, for a brief discussion of Levinas' concept of the "face" and for an extensive note on Levinas' work.

⁵Margery Williams Bianco, *The Velveteen Rabbit* (New York: Avon Books, 1975).

⁶Of course, it is also possible to put a coin in the man's cup and still not see his face. Christina did see his face, and when we returned to Pittsburgh after living in southern California for five years, she wanted to see him again.

⁷See Robert Kegan's *The Evolving Self: Problem and Process in Human Development* (Cambridge: Harvard University Press, 1982) for a discussion of the dance between the "individual" and its "holding community" that is the rhythm of the self.

⁸See John McDargh, "Emerson and the Life of the Self: A Psychoanalytic Conversation," in *The Endangered Self*, Richard Fenn, ed. (Princeton: Center for Religion, Self and Society, Princeton Theological Seminary, 1992), pp. 7–20.

⁹Feminist theologians have effectively revealed how the experience of "having" bodies can be distorted into a mind-body dualism that can see the "true self" as not identical with (or in more overt form in bondage within) our bodies—and how dangerous this tendency can be for the well-being of ourselves and our planet. My statement is not meant to enhance this dualism, only to note that this experience is a piece of the human condition as we have inherited it.

¹⁰See Barbara Kingsolver's essay "High Tide in Tucson" from her book of the same title (New York: HarperCollins, 1995) for a lyrical exploration of how rhythms (like those of the response of a hermit crab to the tide—even when that crab is in Tucson!) are a part of life.

¹¹For a lovely example of this difficulty, see John Irving's *A Prayer for Owen Meany* (New York: Ballantine Books, 1989), pp. 84–87.

Chapter 3

The Mystery of Sin

To want to give a logical explanation of the coming of sin into the world is a stupidity that can occur only to people who are comically worried about finding an explanation.

—Søren Kierkegaard[1]

How can we begin to talk about sin, keeping in mind the reality that life is structured in such a way that ambiguity, conflict, finitude, and suffering are often just a piece of life and that innocence eludes us? How can we talk about sin, honoring Kierkegaard's caution against seeking logical explanations for sin—explanations that might erode both the mystery of sin and our human responsibility for it that he feared a logical explanation for sin could undermine? I would like to suggest five aspects of sin that need to inform our conversation.

Sin That Precedes Us—Inherited Sin
If we start with an understanding of sin as *the violation of others and the earth for which we are responsible* (the violation of the command to love our neighbors as ourselves—Mark 12:31), then we each are born into a world where sin already exists, by which we are affected, and with which we are infected. This is one way the tradition has talked about sin as inherited or original. Even before we are aware of it, sin becomes a part of us. This happens as we participate in social structures that are rooted in injustice. Being born into a North American culture that consumes more than its share of the earth's resources, for example, directly implicates us in sin (although we could argue that it implicates those who are rich more than it

28

does those who are not!). Our lifestyle violates the well-being of others. It is reflected in our language, as our contemporary struggle with inclusive language has painfully revealed to us. We can see it in our national struggle to break out of old assumptions and to discern a responsible relationship with our natural habitat. And we can see it in the privileges that accrue to some of us simply because we were born white in a world that values white people and subordinates people of color. A white student who had always been active in justice causes—particularly the struggle for civil rights for African Americans in this country—traveled one summer to Africa. There she discovered to her horror that she was—without her approval—treated "like a god" and set apart, simply because of the color of her skin. She returned to this country newly sensitized to watch for all the ways she inadvertently participated in and received the fruits of structuralized racism in her own city.

This sin that precedes us and becomes a part of us can be seen as well in inherited sorrow and hate. During our trip to the Middle East, one of our Palestinian friends pointed out to us the village from which his grandfather had come. The grandfather had been forcibly removed from the village by Israeli soldiers and sent to another "recognized" one where he had lived out his life. This friend now lives in East Jerusalem. He loves this city and has no desire to live in his grandfather's Arab village. Still the violation against his grandfather burns inside him, calling for justice. The Capulets hate the Montagues, the Anglos hate the Puerto Ricans, and Romeo and Juliet lie dead in each other's arms.

Inherited sin can be seen wherever a blessed rage for justice does battle with the entrenched forces of the status quo. And its echoes can be heard when the desire for justice has been extinguished, where people born into generation after generation of oppression have so identified with their oppressor that parents now teach their children the oppressor's ways—the Chinese custom of mothers binding the feet of their daughters is an example of such a cycle of oppression. Its echoes can be heard where unjust systems have been "ontologized," granted the favor of a "sacred canopy"[2]—renaming oppression as the natural order of creation, creating a catechism where oppressed and oppressors alike memorize their "god-given" roles, and obfuscating its origin as rationalization for a structure of life that advantages some at the expense of others. One of the first tasks of the feminist movement, for example, has been to expose as a human construction the system of gender assignments characteristic of a patriarchal system. (Of course, parents may sometimes *choose* to teach their children how to survive in the world of the oppressor by showing them how to give the oppressor what the oppressor expects. While this may *look* like an internalization of the oppressor's ideology, and thus a perpetuation of the cycle of sin, it is better named an act of resistance. We'll examine this more thoroughly in the final chapters.)

Inherited sin can be seen vividly wherever apartheid is in place and where even children learn its ways. When I was a child, our family often visited our relatives in the South for Thanksgiving. Once when we were at a shopping mall, I was eating a particularly sticky piece of candy and needed a drink of water. Spying a water fountain against the wall, I walked over to it only to discover that there were two water fountains: one marked colored, the other marked white. I decided to drink out of the one with the colored water! Only after pushing the button on the fountain did I realize that a "colored fountain" was not about rainbows, but about segregation. And I was embarrassed for having drunk out of the "wrong" fountain.

Finally, inherited sin, we now suspect or are forced to consider, can be transmitted to us in our genetic code—witnessed, for example, in violence and rage that could be vestiges of a time when acts of violence were needed to guarantee human survival (which in some situations they can be still). To call such inherited traits sinful, of course, is to suggest that our genetic code does not fully determine our behavior—that environment and choice and human responsibility are also a factor. Or as Marjorie Suchocki has suggested, perhaps these traits are appropriately named "sinful" only when there is a possibility of behaving in another way—when we have an option other than violent activity—that would then transform our inherited tendency to "violence" into "unnecessary violence."[3] Acknowledging how we inherit traits from our ancestors that have become outmoded (no longer necessary for survival) and perhaps at times dangerous, Barbara Kingsolver challenges:

> We humans have to grant the presence of some past adaptations, even in their unforgivable extremes, if only to admit they are permanent rocks in the stream we're obliged to navigate....A thousand anachronisms dance down the strands of our DNA from a hidebound tribal past, guiding us toward the glories of survival, and some vainglories as well. If we resent being bound by these ropes, the best hope is to seize them out like snakes, by the throat, look them in the eye and own up to their venom.[4]

To speak of these traits as inherited sin is one way to "own up to their venom" and to express an awareness that some other behavior is both possible and appropriate.

Conscientization—Naming Our Defenses

Sin in everyday parlance conjures up acts of naughtiness, perhaps even wickedness. We trivialize the word when we say that eating too many cookies is a sin. But we also say that it is sinful when neighbors fail to respond to a dying woman's cry for help, or when a young man is killed by a drunken driver.

When we speak *theologically* about sin, however, we are speaking about more than acts of sin. We are also talking about a state of consciousness—an awareness that one has fallen short of the mark, that one has intentionally or perhaps unwittingly participated in the violation of other human beings. It is a state where the layers of rationalization, denial, innocence, and deceit are gradually peeled away and one is able to see one's actions, one's complicity in structures of violence, with brutal clarity. The story of Oscar Romero illustrates such conscientization.

Oscar Romero was not a bad man. In fact, he was a rather benign man—a scholar, a priest who was chosen to become the Archbishop of El Salvador not because of his leadership skills or his wisdom or his compassion, but because he was perceived by those in power to be one who would be more interested in his books than in the struggles for justice that were irrupting in his country, and more likely to avoid conflict than to encourage it. At first, this much was true. But the more Romero saw the suffering of the peasant people of El Salvador, the more he was able to see both the injustice that caused that suffering and the complicity of his church in that injustice. He then became a passionate prophet, equating the suffering of the people with the suffering of the crucified Christ, who also died a victim of the sins of the world, and calling his fellow Salvadorans to see and confess their sins and begin the task of justice-making.

To see our sin is to see how our privilege, or our need to have everything remain the secure way it has always been, has blinded us to our sin. Father John graduated from seminary ready to save the world and with the assumption that he knew exactly how to do it. Unaware of the presuppositions of hierarchy and power that informed his expectations for ministry, he headed off to his first parish in rural Mexico. So sure was he of his own omnipotence (or, we might say, so ignorant was he of his limits—his humanity), Father John ignored all the warnings he had received not to drink the local water without first boiling it. Within two days, Father John was flat on his back, weakened by dysentery, and dependent upon his parishioners to care for him—even to clean his filthy body and soiled sheets. His ministry began not with him in control and "serving" the people, but with his parishioners taking care of him. This experience revealed to him the prideful (and therefore sinful) assumptions about the power of his position that had shaped both his expectations about the priesthood and his denial of his human frailties that had allowed him to think of himself as "set apart." It also awakened in him a desire to find a new model of ministry—one that recognized the mutual service between pastor and laity and affirmed his new experience of power—not as power over or even as power for, but as power with others.

To begin to see one's sin is not an easy thing. Scrooge, whose miserly behavior is so obviously sinful to the reader of Dickens' *A Christmas Carol*, needs three nighttime visitors before he can awaken to his own treachery. Those of us who are "advantaged" are often well defended against seeing the ways in which our advantage comes at the expense of others (and thus also realizing how fragile that advantage is). We are dependent upon the victims of our sin—those who make our advantage possible—to reveal to us the folly (and probably violence) of our ways. Yertle the Turtle, Dr. Seuss's greedy turtle in the tale by the same name, was so intent upon becoming ruler of all there was to see (much of which, like the moon and the stars, were obviously beyond his control), that he was impervious to the misery of the other turtles upon whose backs he had to stand in order to rule. It was a turtle named Mack—situated at the bottom of the stack—who finally disturbed Yertle's climb to power, a simple burp that landed Yertle the King right back in the mud from which he had first crawled.[5]

But being the "revealer," the messenger with the bad news, is a dangerous task. People often resist learning that they are responsible for the sufferings of others. Sometimes we respond with denial, refusing to hear what the other has to tell us. Sometimes we respond with violence. The PBS series *Eye on the Prize*, which chronicles the civil rights movement in the United States during the 1950s and '60s, graphically replays the resistance white America offered to African Americans protesting for equal rights. As Martin Luther King, Jr., explained the tactic of nonviolent resistance, its goal was not to create violence (even though violence often resulted from the resistance) but to reveal the violence that segregation had for decades wrought upon the souls of black Americans (and also upon white Americans who were in bondage to their fears and hatred). By forcing the American public to witness the violence of Jim Crow laws, African-American resisters revealed to the nation our sin of segregation. Their action was a call to see our sin and repent, a call to see the humanity in the face of people who had suffered under segregation, a call to respond with a justice that would redeem even the souls of the sinners. Sin is hard to see, harder still to confess; sometimes we would rather kill the one who reveals it to us.

Sometimes, in our complex and interwoven world, the one against whom we sin is a friend, which makes the revelation even harder. Early in the feminist movement, white middle-class feminists were oblivious to the way we drew on our own experiences to speak rather imperialistically for all women. It has been hard to hear the voices of our Asian sisters tell us that "You are not my sister!" or to learn from womanist theologians that sexism is not the only form of oppression women suffer—that for African-American women, it is interwoven with racism and classism, and that white feminism has remained ignorant of this reality, thereby reinforcing it.

I have said in this section that in speaking theologically about sin, we are speaking not only about the sin, but also about the conscientization of the sinner. Paulo Freire in his *Pedagogy of the Oppressed*[6] shows how the process of conscientization is also the process of the sinned-against, the coming to awareness of the victims of sin that they in fact live in oppression, and that what they have been given as "the way things are" or "the will of God" is in actuality the result of human-made structures of oppression built to secure the well-being of a few at the expense of the many.

Conscientization is a process of seeing—an "Aha!" experience—that presupposes one has been enabled to see in a new way. Perhaps this "Aha!" happens in a group[7] as one is slowly "heard into speech."[8] Or perhaps it is in a classroom where the class slowly peels away their presuppositions to discover what lies beneath. Or in a therapist's office when the therapist suddenly realizes that all his clients from the same place of employment (describing remarkably similar symptoms of distress) are not crazy but bear symptoms of working in a brutal system. Or when someone refuses to respond with the anger we expect but rather greets us with a love so unexpected that our defenses are momentarily exposed for what they are. Or when we "walk a mile in the shoes" of our enemies only to discover how like us they really are, or how much our ways have threatened them, and how we ourselves are the guilty ones for having constructed them as alien and threatening to our ways.

These "Aha!" experiences speak of the possibility of knowing something in a new way. This is the possibility of grace. From a faith perspective, we can call this the grace of God—God's gift to us that is mediated to us in the ways suggested above. Thus, to speak *theologically* about sin is to affirm that grace (the possibility of a new way of seeing and being) precedes our awareness of ourselves as sinners. In the light of the new, we can see the treachery of the old; in the promise of the new, we are free to repent, confess, and even become in a new way. When we as Christians are called to confess our sins in church each Sunday, we are first reminded of the grace of

God, who loves us so much that we are freed to see our sins and to name them. In a real sense, then, our prayers of confession can be understood as prayers of thanksgiving and hope that God might be working—even in us—a new thing.

Sin Against God and Ourselves

We have spoken about sin as acts of violence against others and our world. As Marjorie Suchocki has provocatively suggested, in our world this is probably the first place where we are likely to see and name our sin.[9] But the command to love our neighbors actually has three parts to it: to love *God* and to love our *neighbors* as *ourselves*. So sin is also against God and ourselves.

In the previous section, I discussed how our awareness of sin is always in the context of God's prior grace, which makes possible to us, in some mediated way, a new way of being or of seeing our neighbor or the structures that support our particular worldview, our way of being in the world. In the light of this new possibility, we are able to see the constricted or sinful way of the old. (This is not to suggest that all "old" is bad. Much of who we become in a new way is constructed out of the old. What I am suggesting is that we come to see our relationship to the old in a new way.)

But as human creatures, we are also free to reject God's possibility for our lives. We are free to continue to participate in systems that violate others for the sake of our own advantage. We are free to believe rather Eeyore-like that we (and/or our world) are "pathetic" and will always be, that no new word can be spoken to us.[10] (This is what the tradition has referred to as the sin of sloth or despair.[11]) We are free to reject the possibility of a love that might expand us, but leave us more vulnerable. We are free to deny that tortures happen, that people are raped, that children are abused, that we are alcoholic or anorexic or worthy of love. We are free to turn from the face of the other—as I did from that homeless man. We are free to be so overresponsible for all the problems in the world that we become hopeless ourselves. And when we in our freedom reject that new possibility from God, then we sin against God as well.[12] And when our refusal of God's new possibility means that we do not see our sin and persist instead in our ways of violation and alienation, then we sin against God, who—we claim in faith—so loves the world that even the hairs on our heads are numbered.

But sin is also against ourselves, for in denying God's new possibility, we also deny what is our own best possibility. And in living in old ways that have constrained our souls, then we sin against ourselves as well. The story of the prodigal son (Luke 15:11–32) reflects this awareness. The son, we remember, decides to leave home and go off into the world. Taking his inheritance (requested prematurely and without even so much as a thank you), the son ventures off into a far country where he loses himself in "the good life." And when his money runs out—as well as his friends and their good times—he finds a job feeding the pigs to support himself. He even ends up eating with the pigs. It is in this space of despair and degradation that a new thought comes to him. He sees his misery and degradation and says to himself, "I could have a better life than this as a mere servant in my father's home. I will return home and tell my father that I have sinned against him by my thoughtless behavior and ask him to hire me on as a servant." Something new has broken through to him—he has seen the folly of his ways *and* his degradation *and* he realizes that he should not/need not live in degradation. He has seen his own self-violation and the disregard for his father that his behavior expressed. So he returns home in a spirit of contrition, but he is not met with judgment. The judgment he has wrought upon himself seems to be sufficient, or not even necessary for the father. Rather, the son is met with joy and compassion. In the context of this love—this second new thing that he learns—he can see on his father's face that his degradation was also his father's degradation, that his "coming to himself" also returns him home, and that the home to which he returns is a different home, one from which a father has dared to run in order to welcome the prodigal back. As sin is also against ourselves and God, so God's grace transforms us and spirals back to affect God as well.

Creation's Complicity and the Tragic Trajectory of Sin

In speaking about sin, the Christian tradition has struggled with the notion that sin is in some way original to the human condition. By original it has meant inherited, something in which we participate even before we are aware of it—an aspect of sin we have already discussed in an earlier section. By original sin, the tradition has also meant that as human beings we universally miss the mark of our full humanity and that our failure seems inevitable. Instead of loving God and neighbor as self, we turn in on ourselves in self-centered concern. This self-concern then tinges everything that we do, so that even our best actions are infected with it. As this intuition of original sin has been developed through the Augustinian strand of the tradition, it has been described as an inherited situation in which human beings "cannot not sin"—a bondage of the will that has worked its way into the Calvinist tradition as the notion of "total depravity." Moreover, this bondage has been understood to be reflected in the divided self that Paul describes in Romans 7 as a self that on the one hand knows the good, but on the other cannot do it. This division within the self (and against the self) is part of the experience of bondage.

There are several problems with the notion of original sin. Most obviously, it can sound as if creation is originally sinful—thereby blaming God for this predicament. But, by linking the word *original* with sin, the tradition has meant just the opposite: it is not our original nature that is sinful. It is our nature *as human beings have shaped it*—perhaps even in our mother's wombs—that is distorted by sin. Original sin, then, is not God's responsibility but the result of human fault—and is tied (in the Augustinian track) back to an original Fall wherein human creatures, created with the possibility to choose the good, by their own choice forfeited that possibility for themselves and for their posterity. But this leads then to several questions: Why would those first creatures have fallen if life in the garden was so perfect? How is this condition communicated? How can human creatures, who are born into a sinful condition, be held responsible for that sin? What is the nature of a God who would punish an entire race for the sin of two people? When we spoke earlier of inherited sin, we saw how one could participate, even unconsciously, in the sin of the world. Because we are complicit in sin in this way, even if we are unaware of our sin, we can be said to be responsible. But if we inherit from our parents the inability not to sin, as if it were in our genes, then how are we to be held responsible at all?[13]

One way to address this problem has been to transform the doctrine of original sin from one that is *prescriptive* (human beings have no choice but to act in this way—or human beings can choose, but do not have a will that can act on that choice) to one that is *descriptive* of human behavior (universally, human beings do act in this way)—and to reinterpret "the fall" from being something that happened at the beginning of time, to a situation that happens universally to each human being. But if "depravity" is not something that we inherit but rather something into which we all seem universally to fall, how can we explain this phenomenon? Why would human creatures, generation after generation, fall inevitably into sin? If the doctrine of original sin no longer means that we inherit the inability not to sin, could we then choose not to sin? Are we, that is, back into the Pelagian controversy? And is there more at work here than the fact that we are born into a world where sin precedes us and into which we are co-opted by the very structures of society into which we are born, to explain what we have called original sin?

What I have called the theologians of the tragic have answered this question with the suggestion that creation (and, by implication, God as well) is complicit in human sin. This is not to say that anything "makes" us sin, but that creation with the diversity, conflict,

ambiguity, finitude, vulnerability, freedom, death, and possibility
that are built into it (a situation we described in chapter 1) is itself
the precondition for sin. This is the initial insight of Søren
Kierkegaard: that life itself, examined (if this is really possible) apart
from what we have been calling inherited sin, is so structured that it
presents human creatures in our finitude and freedom with a condition of anxiety that begs for resolution. Sin is the human response to
a creation that feels, both in its possibility and in its limitation, less
than secure. It reflects an understandable human desire for "safe
passage," for a way to feel secure in a world that threatens that security. It is a response that—made repeatedly—slowly shapes us into
a posture of self-securing from which it becomes more and more
difficult to choose not to sin.[14] Sin in this sense is the human refusal
to accept and live within the anxiety-building parameters of the
human condition and the practice of securing ourselves in ways that
are idolatrous and have grave implications for ourselves, others, and
our world. If life challenges us to live within our parameters (which,
of course, given our freedom, are relatively flexible parameters) and
to trust in the source of this life to secure us, then sin is a refusal of
that trust.[15]

Frederick Buechner, in his book *Telling Secrets,* tells of how his
own life followed this tragic trajectory. Suffering in his childhood the
loss of his father, Buechner knew too well the vulnerability of the
human situation. And so he decided as an adult to make his life more
secure so that he would not have to suffer such a devastating loss
again. Some of us might seek to secure ourselves against life's fragility by not daring to love another, not allowing ourselves to care about
the world, thereby not risking disappointment and loss. Buechner
decided instead to build an idyllic life, one that would be safe for
himself and for his wife and three daughters. This is an understandable desire—which one of us would not want the ones we love to be
safe? But life is not that simple, and our understandable desire to
protect can turn on itself, draining life out of that which it would
protect. (I am reminded of a friend who once covered her lovely
bittersweet bush in all its red-orange autumn glory with plastic bags
in order to keep the birds from eating the berries. The berries lasted
all fall, but the next year, her bush failed to bloom.) And so, Buechner
came face to face with his daughter's anorexia—a condition that was
not only his daughter's, but also his own. As he relates his story:

> During the time of my daughter's sickness and its
> aftermath…I began to understand that though in many ways
> we were both a lucky and loving family, my daughter's anorexia
> was only the most visible manifestation of a complex, subter-

ranean malaise that we were all five of us suffering from—myself maybe most of all. The craving to be free and independent on the one hand and to be taken care of and safe on the other were as much mine as they were my daughter's. Beneath the question about food, there were for her unspoken questions about love, trust, fear, loss, separation, and these were also my questions. Childhood fears persist in us all, and what I feared most was losing what I loved the way years before I had lost a father I hardly knew well enough to love. So I clung onto my children for dear life because in many ways, too many ways, they were my life. I looked to them and to my wife to fill empty places in me which, with their own lives to live, they didn't have either the wherewithal or the inclination to do. I got so caught up in my daughter's slow starvation that I wasn't aware of the extent to which I myself was starving.[16]

To be human, as I said at the end of the last chapter, is to seek anchors in the pulling and tearing of life. Buechner secured himself by holding on to his family for dear life. Others of us may secure ourselves in different ways—through career, fame, wealth, possession, physical fitness, commitment to a certain political ideology, belonging to the right group—even loyalty to a particular faith system. To desire to be anchored seems to me to be a perfectly understandable desire. Yet, the things at hand[17] to which we can anchor ourselves are not themselves ultimate and thus are incapable of truly securing us. We may even in the deepest places in our hearts despair that there is anything that can be ultimate—that in our changing and threatened existence there is anything we can count on.

If the life we are given calls us to live courageously within our vulnerability, to care passionately for ourselves and those we love, yet to love with an open hand, realizing that others must breathe and have their own lives (which includes the freedom not to love us in return—or to grow up and leave us, even though they do love us), then often that courage escapes us. If the life we are given calls us to risk our possibility in a world over which we have only marginal control, then sometimes it seems safer not to risk—or to strive to have control so that our risk is marginal.

And so we sin. We refuse the vulnerability of our human situation (refusing, that is, to be who we are). We build for ourselves structures of our own securing and defend those structures as if our lives depended upon them (which we are convinced they do), thereby distorting those structures (or relationships) beyond any form of pleasure or moderate securing they might offer us. We become captives of our own structures and construct ourselves in conformity to those structures, becoming alienated from ourselves. We violate the face of the one who would greet us or need us along the way, corrupting our relationships with others and the world, thus also becoming alienated from others.

So intent do we become on securing ourselves and those we love that we fail to learn that loving and letting go is not only scary but also the way life works. If our experience of God is somehow possible through the thresholds of our possibility and vulnerability (both of which may be times when we experience that life has a "more than" quality to it), then in our self-securing (whether that is the striving to be all we can be *as if our life depended on it* or defending ourselves against all forms of vulnerability), we also squeeze out the possibility of that "something more."

Our sin, then, has many layers. It is the refusal to be who we are (our refusal to accept our humanity with all our possibility and vulnerability). It is the way that refusal becomes sedimented into postures of refusal (our defensive measures to bolster that which we choose to secure us).[18] It is the way that refusal means the violation of other lives as well as our own (as we use those lives to secure our own). And it is the refusal of the possibility of that "something more" (both God, the source of that something more, and the something more that we might become). This sin, moreover, is never merely our own. It becomes sedimented not only in our own lives, but in the lives of those we touch and in the structures we build and/or in which we participate. It becomes part of our legacy for the next generation—a legacy of inherited sin.

Our Sin Has Many Forms

Sin, we have said, is a basic refusal of our human vulnerability and possibility. It is reflected in all the attempts—inherited and self-generated—to make our lives more secure than they can be, most often at the expense of others, but also at the expense of our own vitality, our own ability to love in an open-handed way, our own sense of wonder and appreciation for the fragile beauty that is a piece of life. Frederick Buechner sought to deal with the fragility of the human condition by bolstering himself and his family against it—creating a fortress of safety. This is one example of what the tradition has called the sin of pride—seeking to be "like God," in control of one's own destiny.

I was raised to think of sin as disobedience, pride, or rebellion. This definition was explained to me through the story of Adam and Eve recorded in Genesis 2 and 3 as it has been refracted through the Augustinian tradition.[19] Whether the story of a primal fall (the true Augustinian position) or the universal story of all human beings, the narrative went something like this. God formed the first creature, Adam, out of the dust of the earth, breathed into him the breath of life, placed him in the garden which he was to till and keep, and told him to enjoy the garden—but not to eat of the tree of the knowledge of good and evil, for then he would die. But Adam was lonely in the garden, and this was not good (the only thing in creation that we are told was not good). So, after creating all the creatures of the earth, none of which satisfied Adam's loneliness, God caused Adam to fall into a deep sleep, and took out of his side a rib, from which God created Eve. And Adam and Eve were delighted with one another.

Now the garden was also inhabited by a serpent—a rather wily creature, who happened upon Eve one day and tempted her to eat the forbidden fruit. Eve resisted at first, knowing God's prohibition. But the serpent was persistent, and Eve eventually succumbed to his argument. She then gave Adam the fruit, which he took without argument and ate. And then craziness broke loose. The two saw what they had done, realized they were naked, and hid themselves. When confronted by God, Adam blamed Eve, she blamed the serpent, and all of creation suffers. They were expelled from the garden, and life became a struggle full of pain and alienation. The wages of sin, I was told, were suffering and death and a bondage to sin from which human beings cannot free themselves.

Now there is much to be said for this rendition of the doctrine of sin. It is a tidy explanation for suffering and death (except for the questions raised earlier about why God would punish all of creation for the sin of two creatures). It reflects the reality that humans do turn from God, that we do blame each other, and that life often is full of struggle and alienation. It also describes what for many is *the* human struggle to be independent, self-made, and autonomous, and warns that human beings are created to be dependent on God and in community with one another.

But we can also sin—inappropriately secure ourselves—by choosing to avoid the risks of life that, by introducing possibility into a more predictable existence, could threaten our understanding of life as we have known it (thus introducing the possibility both of chaos and of a deeper understanding), disrupt the relationships we have carefully held in a certain order, enhance a discontent (a desire for something more) that we may have kept suppressed, or remind us that the basic reality about life is that it changes.

We can avoid this vulnerability of possibility in our life in many ways. We can refuse to move outside our immediate circle of associates, choosing to know only those who are like us and thereby separating "us" from "them." We can avoid possibility by losing ourselves in trivialities or details,[20] or by drowning them, along with life's miseries, in the pursuit of the sensual—thereby distorting our embodied desires, reconstructing them as insatiable.[21] We can reject new responsibilities that might give us the chance not only to develop ourselves, but also to run the risk of failure and of others' seeing our failure.

I have a friend who is wonderfully gifted as a musician. Yet, whenever she has been asked to assume a position of leadership in her church that would make use of these abilities, each time after much inner turmoil she has consistently rejected the possibility. When I asked her why she didn't jump at the opportunity to invest her talents for the good of the whole community—that she might enjoy the rewards of appreciation and self-satisfaction she most likely would receive—she said that she felt better remaining in the shadows where no one had any expectations of her. She'd rather "pop out" of the shadows every once in a while and amaze people with her talent unexpectedly (as when the scheduled pianist failed to show for a worship service one evening), than have her community know how good she could be and expect it of her. Of course, once she had emerged from the shadows her talent was no longer hidden from the community. Her hiddenness, then, fooled only herself.

Sometimes, unfortunately, the possibility of who we are can be one that is not valued by the communities of which we are a part. Not so many years ago, a man who wanted to go to nursing school might have hidden his desire for fear that a "male nurse" would be seen as an anomaly. In our present age, people who discover in themselves a homosexual orientation often haven't felt free to reveal themselves to their communities—so they have hidden themselves, presenting instead a false self that has constrained them from free expression. In these cases, because society has refused to value male nurses or gays and lesbians, we have encouraged them to hide, thus being complicit in their refusal.

We can also avoid the risk of possibility in our own lives by investing ourselves in—even sacrificing ourselves for—the good of others. There surely are times when life demands that we respond to the face of another at some cost to ourselves, but sometimes this sacrificial stance can be used as a cover-up—to hide from ourselves our own possibility (or our own need to be loved in return). We then can expect these others—for whom we have shown such care—to balance the precarious task of becoming themselves *and* securing/ pleasing us in a way that satisfies our needs as well. This sin is treacherous because it often masquerades as love. A mother, determined to devote herself totally to her children's well-being, neglects any form of development for herself. When her children are ready to leave home, she cannot let them go, for they have become her life. In an attempt to nurture them, she actually consumes them, using them to fend off the nagging feeling that she is nobody. Fathers, as Buechner has revealed, can do the same thing. So can those in the helping professions. A minister pours herself out for the good of the community, failing to acknowledge to them and to herself the costs and expectations of such behavior. When her congregation fails to appreciate her in a way she needs, she may then feel burned out and taken for granted.

To talk about the many forms of sin is also to acknowledge that in doing theology, particularly when we are talking about sin, social location matters. Victims and oppressors do not sin in the same way (although the oppressed can choose to oppress others in the pecking order and replicate the sins of their oppressors), nor are they equally accountable for the resulting mess of creation. This means that what appears to be a form of sin in one life may not be sin in another life. For example, we have spoken of one form of sin as pride and control. A person who refuses his vulnerability may try to secure himself by controlling himself and everyone around him. This person may need to repent of his sin and learn to be less in control—to appreciate that he, also, is subject to life's vicissitudes and to learn what there is to learn from that experience.

But victims of another's abuse, who have lived a terrifying existence under another's control (and thereby out of their own control), may need in fact to try to take more control of their lives (for instance, by leaving the abuser)—in awareness of their vulnerability—to defend themselves. To tell the victim that to try to be in control of her own existence (or to be concerned for her own well-being) is sin would in fact be to replicate the violation and increase the sin. Or to tell her that she must care for the face of the other (and what face are they to refer to—the terrorizing face, or the terrified face behind the terrorizer?) rather than attend to her own battered one, is to duplicate the offense. Forms of sin are particular to each situation, and we are dependent upon the grace of conscientization to discern what is sin and what may be a lifesaving (and appropriate and "grace-ful") refusal.[22]

In this section we have talked about the fact that sin takes many forms. We have also reflected the complex situation that sin language needs to be situation-appropriate. We have also raised two peculiar twists on the question of sin. First, we have spoken about how some people hide *at the encouragement (or the refusal) of the society* and yet we have still spoken of their hiding as sin. Is it correct to say that our complicity in the way a society may encourage us to hide is, in fact, sin? Or, is this more a case of blaming the victim for what is actually an understandable survival tactic?[23]

Second, we have heard the question: How do we speak about the behavior of those who are victims of others' sins (be that another individual or a system of oppression)? We have argued that language of sin as pride or control or refusal of vulnerability is not appropriate for these situations. But what language is appropriate to describe a victim's experience of refusal and the postures he or she may assume to replicate that refusal or to resist its repetition?[24] How do we speak about a posture of refusal that results not from one's refusal to accept one's vulnerability (although it may function as a defense against further violation), but from the experience of being refused? And does looking at the doctrine of sin from the perspective of those who have been refused alter any conclusions about sin we have drawn in this chapter? These questions will be the focus of our next section, "Sin and the Broken Heart."

---

[1] Søren Kierkegaard, *The Concept of Anxiety*, p. 49f.

[2] See Peter L. Berger, *The Sacred Canopy*: Elements of a Sociological Theory of Religion (New York: Doubleday, 1967).

[3] Marjorie Suchocki, *The Fall to Violence*, chap. 5.

[4] Barbara Kingsolver, *High Tide in Tucson* (New York: HarperCollins, 1995), p. 8f.

[5] Theodor Seuss Geisel, *Yertle the Turtle, and Other Tales* (New York: Random House, 1958).

[6] Paulo Freire, *Pedagogy of the Oppressed*, trans. by Myra Bergman Ramos (New York: The Seabury Press, 1970).

[7] Judith Plaskow talks about this experience in the context of the women's movement as a "Yeah, Yeah" experience—emphasizing both the experience of conscientization and the group experience of seeing this together. Similarly, conscientization about sin can be both individual and collective. See Plaskow's "The Coming of Lilith" in *Womanspirit Rising:A Feminist Reader in Religion*, Carol Christ and Judith Plaskow, eds. (New York: Harper & Row, 1979), pp. 198–209.

[8] This now classic expression is attributed to Nelle Morton. See "The Dilemma of Celebration" in *Womanspirit Rising*, pp. 159–166.

[9] Suchocki, *The Fall to Violence*, Preface, chap. 2.

[10] Eeyore, of course, is one of the characters in A.A. Milne's *Winnie the Pooh*.

[11] For a discussion of the sin of despair, see Mary Louise Bringle, *Despair: Sickness or Sin?* (Nashville: Abingdon, 1990).

[12] Although as Marjorie Suchocki suggests, writing from the perspective of process theology, God's possibility for us is only a possibility, not a mandate—meaning that this rejection does not carry the sense of disobedience that a more classical rendition of turning from God might conjure. See *Fall to Violence*, chap. 3.

[13] See Farley's discussion of "The Classical Vision of Human Evil" in *Good and Evil*, pp. 124–130.

[14] The best and most current description of this "tragic trajectory of sin" can be found in Edward Farley's *Good and Evil*, pp. 119–138. Farley speaks of the "dynamics" of human evil, and his analysis of this dynamic is the basis for this

section. The language of trajectory is my own. Trajectory is not meant to suggest that there is no choice or responsibility in the development of sin in our lives (that one thing inevitably leads to another). Rather, it is meant to reflect the awareness of those who have become conscious of their sin that there has in fact been a developmental process in that sin—that the posture of refusal did result from initial (and perhaps understandable) and then repeated moments of securing themselves against the vulnerabilities of life.

[15] Farley calls this process the tendency to see the vulnerability of creation as something "sporadic and accidental" and "contingent" rather than accepting it as "necessary and inescapable" (p. 132).

[16] Frederick Buechner, *Telling Secrets* (San Francisco: HarperCollins, 1991), p. 46f.

[17] This phrase resonates with Farley's notion that the "goods at hand " are used to secure us. (*Good and Evil*, p. 134.)

[18] Farley, pp. 130–135, details the "Dynamics of Human Evil" and how they lead to "posture[s] of refusal and insistence."

[19] We have come to realize that Augustine, the principal architect of the classical doctrine of sin, interpreted the human condition—particularly that of guilt and the bondage of the will—through the lens of his own experience. Although his description of the self turned against itself, the self unable to do the right that it willed, is an accurate description of a form of bondage of the will that many human beings suffer, it is not a universal experience, nor—as we shall see in Part II—would everyone necessarily interpret the situation in the same way he did. Rather, it is very probable that Augustine was tormented by a sexual addiction, and that he used this experience of addiction and a body over which he had little control as a metaphor to understand the universal human condition, reflecting—as those of us who might be caught in an addiction know—an addict's sense of powerlessness over his (rebellious) urges, her experience of being divided against herself. For explorations of Augustine's experience see Don Capps's two articles: "Augustine's *Confessions*: The Scourge of Shame and the Silencing of Adeodatus," and "Augustine as Narcissist: of Grandiosity and Shame" found in Donald Capps and James E. Dittes, eds., *The Hunger of the Heart: Reflections on the Confessions of Augustine* (West Lafayette, Indiana: Society for the Scientific Study of Religion Monograph Series, 1990). For a different interpretation see Margaret R.Miles, *Desire and Delight: A New Reading of Augustine's Confessions* (New York: Crossroads, 1992).

[20] This was Valerie Saiving's initial insight to what she argued was a feminine aspect of sin. See "The Human Situation: a Feminine View," in *Womanspirit Rising*, pp. 25–42.

[21] This was Reinhold Niebuhr's insight into the sin of sensuality. See *The Nature and Destiny of Man*, Vol. 1 (New York: Charles Scribner's Sons, 1941, 1964).

[22] Theologians writing from the perspective of abusive family systems have argued that our traditional language for sin doesn't appropriately address those caught in these systems. For example, the understanding of sin as alienation from others, which implies reconciliation as its antidote, is not helpful to women in abusive relationships who may need to separate themselves from these systems, alienating themselves from their partners. See Mary Potter Engel's article "Evil, Sin and Violation of the Vulnerable," in *Lift Every Voice*, M.P. Engel and S.B. Thistlethwaite, eds. (San Francisco: Harper, 1990), pp. 152–164; and Susan Brook Thistlethwaite's critique of feminist writing on sin in *Sex, Race and God: Christian Feminism in Black and White* (New York: Crossroads, 1989), chap. 5.

[23] Moreover, liberation theologians have argued that when our talk about sin focuses on individual sins—whether pride and rebellion or hiding—we miss

the reality of social systems that are structured in sin and continually replicate themselves.

[24] Andrew Sung Park, in *The Wounded Heart of God* (Nashville: Abingdon Press, 1993) has argued that what best describes the situation of the victim is not language of sin but of *han,* which is the experience of violation and the resulting resentment and despair that can accompany that violation—especially when the cycle of violation has been repeated for several generations.

Life batters and shapes us in all sorts of ways before it's done, but those original selves which we were born with and which I believe we continue in some measure to be no matter what are selves which still echo with the holiness of their origin. I believe that what Genesis suggests is that this original self, with the print of God's thumb still upon it, is the most essential part of who we are and is buried deep in all of us as a source of wisdom and strength and healing which we can draw upon or, with our terrible freedom, not draw upon as we choose....

This is the self we are born with, and then of course the world does its work. Starting with the rather too pretty young woman, say, and the charming but rather unstable young man who together know no more about being parents than they do about the far side of the moon, the

Part II

SIN AND THE BROKEN HEART:

The Possibility of Being Refused

*world sets in to making us into
what the world would like us to
be, and because we have to survive
after all, we try to make ourselves
into something that we hope the
world will like better than it
apparently did the selves we
originally were. That is the story
of all our lives, needless to say,
and in the process of living out
that story, the original, shimmer-
ing self gets buried so deep that
most of us end up hardly living
out of it at all. Instead we live out
all the other selves which we are
constantly putting on and taking
off like coats and hats against the
world's weather.*
Frederick Buechner[1]

Introduction to
Part II

W e have seen in the first section of this book that the life we
are given as human beings is one that pulls and tears at us
in many directions. We human beings have the capacity for great
joy, and for a despair that threatens our very souls. We can know
exciting and terrifying possibilities, yet we know those possibilities
within the context of real limits. We are embodied with all the
rhythms, needs, and drives that come with bodies, and we know
the satisfaction of having those needs met, the reality of our
embeddedness in the natural world, the fact of feelings that connect
us to one another (and which can be misinterpreted or overlooked
entirely)—and the ultimate limit of death. We are relational to the
core of our being—and this relationality is both the context for great
richness and the source of great vulnerability.

It is in the crucible of this life, we have said, that we sin. Human
beings seek to secure our unsecured existence, choosing to anchor
ourselves to something (to possessions, relationships, ideologies,
career, etc.) that can secure us and make us safe. Because these things
are unable ultimately to make us safe, we then need to bolster and
defend them. And so we find ourselves in a sort of bondage to that
which would secure us. A refusal of our vulnerability has led to
what Ed Farley has called established postures of refusal that are
not benign. From these postures we are capable of great violence,
rationalization, and deceit in order to keep ourselves secure. Ironically, the more we have to bolster and defend that which we want to
secure us, the less secure we feel and the less freedom we have to
enjoy; the less we are able to appropriately appreciate the partial or
imperfect ways in which life can and does secure us; and the less
capable we are of living into the "something more," within us and
beyond us, that would keep us "all right."

But we have also seen how none of us has been born into a "pristine" insecurity, marked only by the vulnerabilities of the structure of our condition. Rather, we have all been born into a world that is already marred by sin. We inherit this sin, incorporating it into ourselves much like city-dwellers breathe in smog as if it were only air. Structures of sin precede us, and we are taught their ways. The world, in this sense, is fallen. And just by being born, we inherit that fallenness. This is also the human condition.

But the "that's life" quality of the life we are given, the human propensity to secure ourselves which leads us to postures of refusal and denial, our inheritance of sin—these three are not all there is to the human story of sin. In the two paragraphs that introduce this section, we hear again the voice of Frederick Buechner calling us to reflect one more time upon the situation of the lives we have been given. Consider, he says, not only how the structures of our human life pull and tear at us, but also how our most important, life-forming relationships can damage us—demanding of us something that "because we have to survive" we learn to give.

If to sin is to refuse our vulnerability and our possibilities and to structure in ourselves postures of refusal, the experience to which Buechner points is the experience of *being refused*. The world, he says (meaning here mostly his family), rejects the "selves we originally were" and demands (or suggests by threatening us where we are most vulnerable, with the loss of acceptance) that we become something that "the world will like better." And so, as he aptly describes this situation of alienation from self and other, we human beings "live out all the other selves which we are constantly putting on and taking off like coats and hats against the world's weather." Having been refused, we also structure in ourselves postures of refusal that are our defenses against a refusing world.

Rita Nakashima Brock, in her book *Journeys by Heart*, names this experience of being refused *brokenheartedness*. If to be human is to have heart—to have possibilities for life-giving and life-receiving connections that are the ground of the erotic power for life within us—then the damage wrought by being refused is well imaged as the broken heart.[2]

Brokenheartedness—the experience of being refused—happens all around us in our culture. We can see it in structures of racism that deny the full humanity of people of color. (One African-American student once explained to his classmates that racism meant for him getting up in the morning, looking in the mirror, and realizing again that he had to live this day behind "this face.") We can see evidence of it in the behavior of children of immigrants, who go to great lengths to avoid bringing friends home after school because they are ashamed of their ethnic origins. We know it in the sexist structures we have all inherited that have assigned each of us gender roles—naming some human attributes male and others female. As we have felt the pressure to construct ourselves around these gender roles, we have by definition been refused. The little boy who takes his tears to the hiddenness of his bedroom where he can cry alone because he has learned that "big boys don't cry," the adolescent girl who literally sits on her test scores in fear that others will think she is too smart and thus not feminine, have already felt the sting of being refused and have learned to structure themselves out of that refusal.

Refusals also happen—as they did for Frederick Buechner—in the context of our most important human relationships. These refusals can be very subtle—inferred in a disinterested gaze, or in parents' inability to understand their child's frustration. They can be blatant, witnessed in overt pressures on a child to conform to a parent's expectation. ("Why didn't you do better on your report card? Didn't you study, for heaven's sake?") They can be violent, as in the case of physical abuse. ("I'm going to whip some sense into that boy!") They can be chronic, as when a parent continues an incestuous relationship with his or her child, refusing to see the betrayal registered on the child's face.

I have chosen to explore, in the next three chapters, three examples of brokenheartedness that result from refusals that happen in the context of formative relationships. We shall look at the phenomena of shame, of children who develop "giftedness" to compensate for the lack of a parent's unconditional love (thereby participating in what I call the dance of the generations, where each generation perpetuates refusals upon the next), and of controlling family systems that turn the dance of life into a march. These are all phenomena that seem to be of interest to North Americans, since the literatures about them currently fill the self-help shelves of our local bookstores. I have chosen them because in this appeal to North American interests I discern a sense that these phenomena are speaking to people about a very real experience and concern that may be their own. Thus, I assume that the experiences of brokenheartedness revealed in these literatures—while not always precisely defined or completely scientific in method—are real for many people.

I further assume that the popularity of this literature may mean that many people who read it could be people who still choose to attend churches regularly—and that those who attend church may do so bearing broken hearts. This situation, then, becomes a theological challenge to our churches—and one worthy of inclusion in our conversation about sin. Brokenheartedness is clearly a state of alienation formed in refusal. Out of brokenheartedness, people do shape for themselves postures of refusal—postures that, we will see, look very much like the postures assumed in the "tragic trajectory of sin." But is brokenheartedness, which is the result not of *refusing* but of *being refused*, sin? Or is it something else? Or is it both sin and not sin? And how can churches—which call people to be forgiven of their sins—also speak to people's broken hearts?

To be human, I have said, is to have the possibility for great joy and loss. Joy suggests jumping, leaping—even dancing for joy. Loss also suggests a dance of sorts in the time-worn processing of grief that eventually leads one back to wholeness. The brokenhearted (and here I mean not those who have suffered loss, but those who have been refused) may also dance. But the dance of alienation danced by the brokenhearted is rarely one of joy or of a process of grief that leads one back to life (although, it may definitely be a dance forged in great grief!). Rather, it may be a dance of compulsion, perfection, busyness, or hiding. It may be an evasive maneuver learned to protect ourselves from being seen. It may be a carefully choreographed attempt to evoke in someone a love that will not reject. It can be a dance of seduction that has no intention of becoming a dance of intimacy.

The next three chapters describe three such dances of alienation. Consider them, then, as a part of our conversation about sin.

---

[1] Frederick Buechner, *Telling Secrets* , p. 44f.

[2] Brock calls this damage sin—by which I believe she means original sin. It is through damage that sin (alienation from our erotic power) is communicated. She then shows how the patriarchal family is such a seedbed of damage. I agree with Brock's project. But because I believe that damage is endemic to the human condition (some damage is inevitable in the regular give-and-take of life) I have chosen not to name damage as sin. Rather, I focus the question of what is sin on the results of the damage—the ways damage is not seen, attended to, and healed, and the ways human beings, having been refused, continue to live out of the refusal by continuing to structure themselves out of that refusal.

Chapter 4

Shame: The Broken Tie That Binds

Like all children, I was occasionally mischievous and misbehaved. In more carefree times my pranks, like my brothers', met with swift punishment from parents who believed that sparing the rod was certain to spoil the child. The occasional token chastisement was easy to resist psychologically. One had only to refuse to apologize and express contrition for enough hours to gain the upper hand on parents who were tired in the evening and wanted to go to bed. Now, however, I encountered more subtle, and to me more terrifying, punishments. If I misbehaved, my parents simply acted as though I were not their child but a stranger. They would inquire civilly as to who I was and what I was doing on Coorain, but no hint of recognition escaped them. This treatment never failed to reduce me to abject contrition. In later life my recurring nightmares were always about my inability to prove to people I knew quite well who I was. I became an unnaturally good child, and accepted uncritically that goodness was required of me if my parents' disappointments in life were ever to be compensated for.

—Jill Ker Conway[1]

We all have painful memories of moments in our childhood when we felt deeply shamed. A choir director speaks sternly to a group of restless children, telling them to sit quietly, but seems to direct her gaze at one child who feels targeted for the group's noisiness. A third-grade class watches a movie on personal hygiene, and one little girl tries very hard to remember when she has last washed her hair—convinced that if the hygienist were to examine her scalp, she would find colonies of the awful bugs so graphically displayed in the film. A father completely forgets, in the midst of his busy work schedule, that he has promised to take his son to a ball game, and the little boy—who has spent the day looking forward to the outing—quickly tries to hide his disappointment and embarrassment for having taken his father's promise so seriously. An adolescent's voice cracks while answering a question in class, and his fellow students erupt in laughter. A girl's body begins to mature, and she seeks to hide the evidence for fear that she will be teased. A child, with abilities beyond those expected for her age, feels as if there is no place for her in her peer group and fears she will always be different from everyone else.

Shaming incidents, unfortunately, do not suddenly disappear when we become adults. A young professional at a planning conference volunteers a new idea—being careful to cover her enthusiasm for it and any evidence of how long she has spent conjuring it—only to have it ignored or ridiculed. An up-and-coming engineer is passed over for a much-deserved promotion. A professor, when asked a question she has never considered, calls the question naive, reinforcing her student's fear of speaking up in class. Your child throws a temper tantrum at the local supermarket, and you have a sudden desire to disappear. Sometimes, as in the story of Jill Ker Conway, shame is even used by those with power over us as a weapon of control. Elizabeth Clark has argued, for instance, that the preaching of the early church fathers was designed precisely to create a panoptical[2] effect—where people would learn to internalize the church's watchful gaze and therefore become effectively viewed and potentially shamed at all times.[3]

In talking about shame, I have chosen to use examples of shaming that might be common to many people because they are so "everyday." However, shame can also be more overt and therefore more damaging, as in the case of physical, sexual, or emotional abuse.[4] Racism, sexism, and poverty, similarly, are systems that have shame structured into them. A young black man, for instance, can talk about how as a child he tried to scrub the darkness off his face in order to be acceptable to a white community. Or a young woman, stuck with her family in a cycle of poverty, both longs to be invited to an elaborate party and fears the same invitation, knowing that she does not own the appropriate clothes for such a party.

Our self-help literatures have taught us to make a distinction between shame and guilt. Guilt, we are told, is feeling bad about something we have done. Shame, on the other hand, is feeling bad about who we are, or—to put it another way—to feel that we (or parts of ourselves) *are* bad. Whether guilt and shame truly are two different human experiences (it seems to me that they actually bleed into one another), the present literature on shame raises to our consciousness a feeling about ourselves and our worthiness that most of us would rather not talk about. As Gershen Kaufman describes the experience:

> All of us embrace a common humanity in which we search for meaning in living, for essentially belonging with others, and for valuing of who we are as unique individuals. We need to feel that we are worthwhile in some especial way, as well as whole inside. We yearn to feel that our lives are useful, that what we do and who we are do matter. Yet times come upon us when doubt creeps inside, as if an inner voice whispers despair. Suddenly, we find ourselves questioning our very worth or adequacy. It may come in any number of ways: "I can't relate to people." "I'm a failure." "Nobody could possibly love me." "I'm inadequate as a man or as a mother." When we have begun to doubt ourselves, and in this way to question the very fabric of our lives, secretly we feel to blame; the deficiency lies within ourselves alone. Where once we stood secure in our personhood, now we feel a mounting inner anguish, a sickness of the soul. This is shame.[5]

In this passage, Kaufman describes not only the experience of shame—a deeply personal experience in which an inner "I" seems to be judging itself in such negative ways—but also points to the roots of shame in the relational bridges between people where "I" begin to suspect that "I" am unlovable. Thus, while shame seems to be about "me," it is never just about "me." It is always something about "me" (not necessarily true) that "I" learn (or infer) from "my" interactions with others in the human community. Within the context of the community, it is an experience of anguish where "I" feel "seen through" and judged deficient, where "I" feel expendable and where the meaning that "I" have invested in myself (and by inference in life) seems very tenuous—almost as if "I" have been excised from the human race.

This experience can be initiated in a number of ways. Often key to initial experiences of shame is the surprise factor. Shame surprises us, it reveals ourselves or our situation to us in a way we haven't seen before. It can happen in situations where we fall short of an established norm or goal (the norm of the community, the goal of a situation, or our personal goal—formed in the context of our community—for who we want to be). A child is the fastest swimmer in her age group, and so she convinces her mother to advance her to the next group. In her first race in this new division, she is eliminated from the competition in the first heat. Falling short of her goal, seeing herself to be not the winner she thought she was, she immediately leaves the scene and considers giving up swimming. A newly ordained minister is invited to sit at the head table at a fund-raising banquet by a parishioner who is chairwoman of the board of the largest corporation in his city. Only after he has finished his fruit cup and salad does he realize that he has used the wrong fork and spoon. He has a sudden desire to disappear under the table. A ten-year-old boy picks up his little sister after school to walk her home. His sister does not cooperate with him, and so he yells at her and threatens to tell on her. At that moment, his favorite teacher walks by and seems surprised to see him yelling at his sister. He decides that she is not his favorite teacher anymore.

Shame happens not only in individual occurrences, but also through shaming systems. These systems don't necessarily have the same surprise factor. Here shame is expected, dreaded, sometimes internalized, and one can learn to navigate around treacherous land mines to avoid shaming situations. For instance, a parent whose race may make her the target of a racist police department may teach her children not to behave in any way that might draw attention to themselves. But one can still be caught by surprise in these systems when the land mine moves, or the boundary is shifted. A daughter who dresses a certain way to please her abusive father can be taken by surprise when his taste suddenly shifts (or a situation demands from him a response different from the one he might make in the privacy of his own home) and he publicly embarrasses her.

We can feel shame when we are rejected or feel the weight of another's disappointment in us that seems to threaten our relational bridge. Sally was an "ideal" student. Her teachers appreciated the way she was always polite and prepared for class. They often asked her to run errands for them during class time, trusting that she would not abuse the opportunity by dallying along the way but would do exactly as she was told. Sally enjoyed her privileged place and valued herself as a student who was thought of so highly. During her senior year in high school, Sally's classmates invited her to participate in planning a class prank. The prank seemed rather innocent and humorous to Sally and she was pleased with the opportunity to be included with her fellow students. She joined in with great enthusiasm. Only afterward did she realize that her participation in the prank diminished her in her teachers' eyes. One teacher stopped Sally in the hall to tell her how disappointed he was in her behavior (a disappointment her classmates didn't share in since the teacher expected such behavior from them!). Sally felt singled out, shamed, and caught between a rock (her teacher's expectations for her, which she valued and didn't want to lose) and a hard place (her desire to be like her friends).

Or we can feel shame when someone else has disappointed us (as in the case of the boy and the ball game). A parent asks his child to leave him alone in his office for a while so he can finish a report on which he is working—not meaning to reject the child, but also not responding in the affirming and accepting manner to which the child has become accustomed. A friend neglects to return a phone call for several days. We send a valentine to someone we have had a crush on for weeks and later find the card in the wastebasket.

Shame can happen when we feel like we do not fit into a group (and this works best if the group is exclusive or elitist). A teenager is selected for her high school cheerleading squad and feels a new boost in self-confidence. This feeling is shattered when—as an order form is passed around for everyone to list shoe-sizes (so that the adviser can order sneakers for the entire squad)—she discovers that her feet are two sizes larger than anyone else's. Feeling set apart and suddenly gawky, she puts down the wrong size, so that she can seem like everyone else. Her sore feet throughout the season, however, only remind her of her inadequacy.

A young man sits in church listening to the pastor preach about the true faith. He has questions about the theology he hears from the pulpit, yet he is afraid to let anyone know, since the pastor has warned the congregation that if they don't believe the truth he speaks, they will not be saved. The young man begins to hate his thoughts (thinking that something must be the matter with him for having them) and fears that if he tells his pastor what he really thinks, he will be rejected. Although this experience has not actually happened between two people but within the young man himself as he envisions a possible rupture in a relationship that has been important to him, the pastor has participated in the shaming experience by creating the expectation in the young man that participation in this relationship is conditioned upon having acceptable thoughts.

Shame can also happen when the rules change and suddenly we find ourselves in a world different from the one in which we have learned to navigate. When I teach about inclusive language, for example, I often think that some students' resistance to hearing the issue ("When I say 'men,' I always mean women, too!") and learning a new way of speaking ("If you mean 'men *and* women,' then why don't you just say it that way and make it explicit!") reflects their shame at being exposed as speaking in an exclusive fashion. No one likes to be told that he or she has been wrong or hurtful to others—especially when such hurt is unintended.

Or shame can happen when we are in fact blamed or overtly shamed. A father who himself was shamed as a boy wanted to make sure that his son did not bring more shame upon him. When his son was very young, he took him to a dentist's office. The son, terrified of all the equipment, especially the drill, refused to cooperate with the dentist—even to the point of biting the dentist's fingers. His father was so embarrassed by his son's behavior that he yanked him out of the chair (without a thought as to why his son had behaved as he had), told him he was a bad boy, and made him apologize to the dentist.

To be human, we have said, is to be relational—dependent upon one another for nurture, recognition, companionship, and support (what Kaufman calls "belonging" and the need to "matter"). We have also said that to be human is to know broken relational bridges, disappointments, conflicts, differences of opinion, times when what we expect is not what we get, times when people misunderstand what we are saying, or when we discover that what we thought mattered is not what matters to everyone at all. To be human is to be vulnerable to shame. Shame is inevitable to the human situation.

While shame is always a painful experience, it can also be a helpful one.[6] It can teach us, for example, when we have pushed a limit too far. When I was ten years old, I was hospitalized for a hernia operation. Apparently I recovered more quickly than the doctor had anticipated. One day, when the ward nurse failed to answer the phone after it had rung for many minutes, I was able to leap from my bed and answer the phone for her in my best imitation of her voice: "Pediatrics ward, Miss Fenton speaking." It was only when the voice on the phone said back to me, "Who is this? Where is Miss Fenton?" that I realized I had crossed a boundary and was sure to be in big trouble.

Shame can also tell us that we are frightened or unsure about ourselves in a certain situation. (The teenager who finds herself tongue-tied when she finally makes a dreaded phone call may be reflecting her own uncertainty about her readiness to make this connection.) It reminds us how fragile our expectations and relationships can be. (This, of course, can be a terrifying experience unless it is also met by a counter experience that some expectations are met or even surpassed and that relationships—though threatened—can still be resilient.) It also shows how easily we move from "what I do" to "who I am" in seeking to evaluate a situation. (The child whose best friend's mother says accusingly to her, "I've got a bone to pick with you" thinks not just "What did I do," but "What has she seen about me that I don't know?")

Shame is a piece of the human experience. But the shame that we are talking about as a dance of alienation is not just this experience of shame. As we have said, shame can be a good thing. And even the shame that is not good can be healed when it is attended to by someone who recognizes its symptoms and cares enough to make sure that the bridge between others that the experience can temporarily close off (leaving the shamed person feeling isolated and deficient, as if he or she doesn't belong to the human race) is repaired.

The shame that is the dance of alienation is shame that has become what John Bradshaw calls "toxic."[7] It is a step beyond the experience of shame to shame that is ongoing, systemic, or left without healing attention. This dance is not usually born of more benign, healed, or single experiences of shame. More than likely it takes shape when shame experiences have been particularly devastating (as in the case of rape or incest), or chronic (where one never heals from an experience of shame but, through repetition, experiences shame as "the way things are"), when shaming has been used repeatedly as a tool for control, when the system in which we live is "shame-based" (one that indoctrinates people as to their unworthiness or that always needs to blame someone or something when anything goes "wrong"), or when the person who shames us is a very significant other in our pantheon of relationships. It reflects not only the external shaming incident(s) but an internal process that is both an inner turmoil that repeats over and over again to the shamed self "I'm inadequate," as well as the compensating strategies we devise to avoid revealing what seem to be our inadequacies and to defend against ever being shamed again. It is a dance of isolation, but a dance born of a broken heart.

To know shame is to experience ourselves as deficient. The dance of alienation that is toxic shame is the process of internalizing that shame and the protective strategies we form to defend ourselves from ever being shamed again. In this dance, what was an experience of shame becomes a core definition of who we are. If shame is an experience of refusal, then toxic shame is one possible dance of refusal.

The Dance of Shame[8]

Robert Gary Dalton was afraid of girls—or at least, that's what everyone at school said. He was one of the brightest boys at school, but as soon as a situation turned social, he would disappear. If a girl spoke to him, he looked at the floor—unable even to excuse himself. Once when a female classmate—unbeknownst to Robert—was visiting his mother, he happened to barge into the living room to ask his mother a question. Seeing the visitor sitting on the sofa, he stopped mid-sentence, turned around, and bounded up the stairs to his room until it was safe to venture out again. Robert was caught in a cycle of shame from which he felt unable to extricate himself.

Gershen Kaufman speaks of the dance of shame as a process of internalization whereby an experience of shame becomes lodged within us as our identity. From an experience of being shamed we learn to think of ourselves as shame. This dance of shame is one of rejection, vigilance, binding, isolation, and defensive postures. If the experience of shame is one that implicates the self as "seen through" and "unworthy," then the dance of shame is one that stores that experience within the self (as a part of our identity)—enhancing our vulnerability to shame so that we no longer need an external shaming experience in order to suffer the agony of shame.

A scholar is excited by a new book in his field. Suddenly, in the midst of his reading, he becomes caught in an internal web of self-accusation and shame. The book has triggered in him a memory of an occasion when he participated in a conference led by the author of the book. At that conference, the scholar had asked a very pointed and angry question of a fellow participant—only to realize immediately afterward that his manner in asking the question had been inappropriately angry and had hurt the feelings of the other person. When the group later gathered around the table, the scholar wanted to free himself from the embarrassment that still clung to him by explaining himself to the group and apologizing to the person he had wounded. The offended participant, however, never returned to the group. And so the scholar returned home from the conference not having had the opportunity to restore the broken bridge and fearing that all the participants must think he was an awful person. (Note how he never checked this out with the other participants. He handled himself throughout the conference as if his conclusions about what other people thought and felt were accurate.)

Now every time the scholar comes upon a reference to one of the participants in that conference, the memory and the accompanying shame overcome him, and he struggles to justify his behavior to himself while at the same time hating himself for having made the mistake he made. There is no one in this struggle within him but himself—yet the experience of shame is as vivid and agonizing as if his office were crowded with observers. Having never resolved the shame experience, he is stuck with it and it paralyzes him, making it hard for him to consider attending future conferences for fear that someone from the original gathering will be present and see right through him again. Shame has become a part of his internal environment. (It is also likely, given the way he failed to check out his perceptions with others but instead allowed them to rumble into a shame spiral, that this experience remained with him because he already had had—before this incident—a series of shaming events that had created in him a core of shame, from which perspective he then participated in the world and evaluated himself.)

This same type of internal shame reaction can be triggered in any number of ways. For instance, driving past our old high school, we can reexperience a painful memory. Or, running into someone at a school reunion who had been present at a particularly embarrassing occasion in one's life (even if that person has no conscious memory of that event, so trivial had it been to her), can rehearse the old feelings. (Of course, checking out the memory with another and discovering that it wasn't the major event we had felt it to be can be a way of restoring our memories to their rightful proportions!) The memory of shameful events is not the issue here. Rather, the concern is the dance of alienation that accompanies the memory, wherein we struggle within ourselves (or perhaps with a new partner with whom we can replay an old struggle) both as we become vigilant watchers who have learned to monitor everything we ourselves do for fear of happening into another shame-inducing incident—thereby functioning both as protectors and as judges—*and* as we suffer again the agony of the shame (which, since no one is around actually to see through us, is an unnecessary activity we perpetrate upon ourselves).

This dance of shame that alternates between accusing and suffering is not benign. When we are caught in it, it can sap the life out of our souls. It also inevitably infects our relationships with others. Dan developed his internal eye at an early age. Perhaps because his native creativity was not appreciated by others, perhaps because his parents were vigilant about themselves—always measuring themselves (but never their children: they were not abusive in this sense) by some unreachable standard they could inevitably see reflected in other people—Dan learned to stifle his creativity (it must be bad!) and to evaluate himself by other people's behavior. Needless to say, his adolescent years were extremely painful as he learned to develop those parts of himself that garnered appreciation and hide those parts that he judged unacceptable. He grew very envious of what appeared to him to be the ease with which others negotiated the perilous journey of a social life. He did not outgrow this dance of alienation, but took it into adulthood and into his marriage. There it could rear its ugly head at social occasions, when Dan would alternately chastise himself for not being more outgoing, feel envious of others for their apparent ease in social situations, and then chastise himself again for being so envious. When these inner cycles hit, Dan became withdrawn from others (which makes sense—all of his energy was directed within). Others then would stop trying to draw him into the conversation, and the isolation he feared would be accomplished (no one made any room for him in the conversation!). This sense of isolation only compounded his inner battle, proving to himself once again his own inadequacy.

Dan's inner dance was toxic not only in social occasions, but also in his relationship with his wife. When he was dancing his inner dance, he would still outwardly perform the functions he thought were expected of him. He still went to work, did his part of the kitchen chores, attended to the garbage, cleaned up after the kids, paid the bills. At times, his inner dance became so much a part of him that he was not even conscious he was doing it—only that he harbored a low-grade but constant sense of dis-ease about himself. Still this dance consumed his energies and left him functioning as a veritable robot (a well-meaning robot, but a robot nonetheless). His wife began to complain that he didn't love her, which seemed ridiculous to him since he knew he did and since he had been performing all his functions in his best effort to be a good husband. But, in fact, he was unable to love her in these moments, so caught was he in his own internal dance of watch and blame, suffer and shame.

Dan's dance of shame was further enhanced by his tendency to blame himself when anything went wrong. Often what "went wrong" was simply an accident, or a result of a natural limitation, but it could send him into his cycle of self-shame. This ability to blame himself developed because, when he was a child and pieces of himself were not accepted, he had *assumed* that this rejection meant that he was *unacceptable*—therefore also assuming that he was to blame for his unacceptability. If the world had refused him, then it must have been his fault. This increased his sense of shame (and also his anger at not being acceptable, which he often turned on himself as anger for his envy of those who were acceptable); but it also protected him from seeing that sometimes those he trusted had in fact let him down. Blaming himself was a way of coping with a world that at times shamed him, thereby making no sense at all. Blaming, and thus shaming himself, was a way he had learned to cope with the world, but it was a way of being that had repercussions both within himself and between himself and his wife. In the one relationship he had hoped would relieve him of his sense of isolation (nurtured in shame—how can one feel connected when so much of oneself is not acceptable?), instead he relived his old agony. He felt at times like an infectious disease. (Important to Dan's isolation, as well, was his inability to be conscious of what he was doing and to communicate what he suffered to his wife. Had he been able to do this, it might have relaxed the cycle of shame

and isolation and begun to show some light on the murky workings of his inner dance.)

Since this dance of shame is obviously extremely painful and
energy-consuming (as we must continually be both watchful of ourselves and vigilant to protect ourselves from situations or other
people that feel dangerously shame-inducing), we can also develop
other strategies to protect ourselves (and, of course, all these strategies are enormously energy-consuming). We can also choose to hide
pieces of ourselves that were particularly vulnerable to shaming by
another, thus binding them with shame (we assume that to experience these pieces of ourselves will shame us), and often purging
them from our consciousness.

Charlotte was raised in a family that paid an inordinate amount
of attention to her emerging sexuality, periodically embarrassing her
as her body assumed new proportions. Her father, with whom she
had been particularly close (and who felt suddenly awkward around
his daughter, not knowing if the rules were changing as to what was
appropriate touching between father and daughter) seemed to with-
draw from her and asked her once not to walk around the house in
her slip when she was getting dressed in the morning because "it
was not fair to him." Feeling ashamed of herself, Charlotte developed a style of dressing that camouflaged her figure—even, from
time to time, binding her breasts with an ace bandage. She became
involved in sports and her classmates called her a "tomboy." When,
despite herself, a young man on the football team found her attrac-
tive and asked her for a date, Charlotte was so worried about what
might happen sexually that she worried herself into a case of diar-
rhea and ended up breaking the date. In later life, she married and
had children, but even when sexual intercourse was pleasurable for
her, she would afterward feel awful about herself—as if a watchful
eye were judging her for her sexuality. (And, indeed, her culture's
watchfulness of women's bodies in general only increased her sense
of needing to monitor herself.)

If we were outspoken, or angry, or sexual—or merely enjoyed
life with an exuberance appropriate to anyone given the gift of life—
and if we were shamed (especially repeatedly) for these attributes,
then it makes sense that we might bind them away to avoid being
shamed again. A graduate student wrote what for her was a life-
changing paper and was encouraged by her professors to seek publication. To her elation, the piece was published. But then, to her
shame, she was castigated by the scholarly community for not adequately footnoting certain classic articles that she actually had not
read before publishing her piece. Duly shamed by a community she
had hoped to impress, she became hesitant to publish any of her

work, finding it easier to focus on her teaching rather than on her publication. A young husband, repeatedly shamed by his father for being "out of line" whenever he became very excited about anything, finds himself becoming "more adult" every time his new wife becomes enthusiastic about her life. An adolescent who has not yet learned to master his newly long limbs fails at youth league soccer and never tries out for a sports team again. As an adult he is uncomfortable when the men in his workplace discuss sporting events over lunch.

Sometimes, as in the case of the graduate student, shaming events remain within the scope of our remembered history and we can actually be aware of the shame bind that paralyzes us. But, at other times, the shaming events can happen at such an early age that parts of ourselves become bound off from ourselves—almost as if we never had them. This bind, and the accompanying underlying sense of ourselves as being deficient (the result of being "seen through" and found wanting), then become a part of our sense of who we are. Our identities are forged in shame, as if shame were not an *event that happened to us* but is actually *who we are*.

If the dance of alienation that is born of shame is one of watchfulness lest anything happen to trigger a shame reaction within us, it also can be an external dance of defensive measures we can assume to protect ourselves from further shaming events. Kaufman lists the following as possible defensive postures: rage, contempt, striving for power, striving for perfection, transfer of blame, and internal withdrawal. Most of these we have already seen as tactics used as the shame cycle spirals deep within oneself. But these postures can also be generated outward, designed to keep others from shaming us again or to shame others before they can shame us, as well as within (protecting the shameful situation from penetrating to our inner core). Caught unprepared for a test on *The Scarlet Letter*, Chris blamed her teacher for not warning her what to expect. Shamed repeatedly when his father caught him off guard, Tony made sure the world, and anyone with whom he came into contact, were under his control. His goal was to move to the top of the hierarchical system in which he worked so that there would be no one above him who could shame him. When he was from time to time caught off guard, he would turn his shame into rage, finding a reason to castigate someone below him on the hierarchical ladder (blaming his secretary for the mistake, or beating his wife because he couldn't beat his boss). Caught by her sister as she tried to sneak a cookie before dinner, Sara turned on her sister in rage, accusing her of being a snoop. Having been publicly ridiculed once for submitting a paper that was hastily written because he had forgotten until the last minute that it was due, Nathan strives never to be shamed again. He becomes intensely judgmental of his own work and feels so vulnerable when he turns in the best paper in his class that he is surprised when a classmate refers to him as a "perfectionist." (Insidiously, perfection is out of reach for any human being in our given limitation. Thus to strive for perfection is to court failure, and to protect against shame in this way is to become more vulnerable to shame in the long run.)[10]

If to be human is to depend upon human relationships for nurture and support and for knowing who we are—if to be human is to long both to love and care for others and to be loved in return, which means risking the possibility of being rejected—then the defensive measures we can adopt to protect us from shame disrupt this fundamental part of our humanity. Relationships that are rather spontaneous and "given" become something we must earn or try to control—or something that we feel is very dangerous. It makes sense then that the dance of shame is often also a dance of isolation. Just as Dan, in spinning within himself, never learned how to dance a dance of intimacy with his wife, so a natural expression of shame is to isolate ourselves from community with others. If shame is a refusal of ourselves, then isolation, it seems, should protect us from ever being shamed again.

But isolation also is a context within which our shame festers. Robert Gary chose to avoid girls rather than suffer a shameful incident. But by protecting himself, he also denied himself the possibility of a relationship that could be fun and rewarding—a relationship in which he might learn that, although at times he could be awkward and embarrass himself, there were also times when he could be warm and witty and receive another's appreciative gaze. In isolation, we might keep the shame spiral under control, successfully avoiding any triggers and living in some semblance of peace. But in isolation the broken bridge of relationality that is the context of shame can never be repaired, and one can never learn a possibility other than the one that was so painful. The shame bind Kaufman speaks of becomes a bind not only because in it we bind parts of ourselves to shame and try to control or disown them, but also because it is a form of bondage from which, alone, we are not able to free ourselves. Indeed, we can see how even our best efforts to manage our pain (through isolation or rage or the quest for perfection) can compound our pain and cut us off from any possible relief.

Blest Be the Tie That Binds: Mending Broken Bridges

We have seen that shame is both the painful human experience of being "seen through," and the process of shaming wherein we learn to think of ourselves (or parts of ourselves) as shameful and to develop dances of shame to protect ourselves from being shamed again. Both the experience and the process result from the rupturing of an interpersonal bridge—a process that both damages the interpersonal bridge and results in the rupturing of the intrapersonal bridge, our process of self-identification. We might suppose then that healing has something to do with rebuilding bridges, with turning shame binds that cut us off from parts of ourselves and others into ties that bind us together with others in the human community. And this, Kaufman argues, is correct.[11]

But healing broken bridges is not easy. On the one hand, as we have seen, people caught in a shame bind tend to avoid connections that could risk further shaming. Thus the opportunity to heal is often missed. On the other hand, once we have been immersed for a long time in our dance of shame, shame has become such a core to our identity that we can forget the interpersonal origin of our shamefulness—forget that the feeling that "I am shameful" results from experiences of "I am shamed." The process of healing, then, has three parts. It is the process of learning to risk again the possibilities and vulnerabilities of relationships with others; of learning that while shame happens, not all relationships are by definition shaming ones; that while relationships can be wounded, they can also be healed; that trust is possible and even viable; and that while we may feel totally shameful, it is possible for someone to love us in our shame, and even believe for us that our shame is not all of who we are. It is a process of remembering what has been forgotten, bringing it into the light where we can examine it for what it is (which means feeling again the pain and humiliation of that shame, grieving the fact that this rupture was never attended to and healed, realizing the damage that we have continued to perpetrate on others and ourselves in our dances of shame, and restoring our knowledge of our shamefulness to its correct place of origin—in a historical event—a rupture between two or more persons and not in some hidden defect). It is also a process of *re*-membering our selves—a bringing together, a reconciliation, of all the pieces of ourselves that we have bound to shame and apart from "us." This is not a linear process; each part folds back into the others until the healing is complete.

Sally had been a precocious child (so she was told)—so it was no surprise that she reached her midlife crisis before she was forty. She had always been a high achiever, always pushing herself to do her best work. She took pride in her lovely polished appearance and in the large number of people in her community who seemed to admire her and respect her work. But inside herself, Sally had a gnawing sense of her own inadequacy.

In midlife—as it later seemed to Sally—all her systems broke down. Her father died and she was overcome with grief. Her sense of inadequacy took over, and she could no longer maintain her self-image of perfection. She feared that the respect she so valued was disappearing from the faces of her friends and colleagues.

Sometimes during this period, when she returned home from work (a job whose challenges she previously had found exciting), Sally could barely pull herself up the stairs to her bedroom. And when she did; she would collapse on her bed, covering her face in an attempt to blot out her growing fears that she was about to become a "bag lady." (This meant to her someone who could not function well, who would become lost in the shadows, and whose face people would glance upon with pity.) She felt full of shame and without the energy to cover it up.

Luckily for her, Sally's job required that she be part of a support group. She had always enjoyed the interactions with her friends in this group. But as her bag-lady fears took a greater grip on her, she began to dread these meetings as well—fearful that she would expose herself and that her friends, seeing her in all her grotesqueness, would recoil in horror. So, for several weeks, Sally participated only marginally with the group. But then one day, as one of her colleagues began to talk about how overwhelmed he felt about fathering his adolescent son, Sally felt tears flowing down her cheeks and heard a sob escape before she could swallow it. Slowly the group's attention turned to her and she felt stuck trying to explain what she didn't understand herself. "I don't know why I'm crying," she said. "Maybe Phil's love for his son reminded me of how much I miss my own father." "Oh," her group leader said, "has your father died? Why didn't you tell us?" And then Sally told the group how she had been afraid to let them see her grief—afraid that her feelings would repulse them.

But Sally's feelings did not repulse her friends. Instead, they gathered their chairs into a tight circle around her and supported her until her crying abated. This was not easy for Sally. Her family had always kept their emotions under control (she'd never seen either her father or her mother cry)—and she had come to think that her tears were ugly. But as she tolerated having her friends see her sad state, she also felt their love cutting through her tears and fears. And she was able to hear them when they said her tears were not ugly but were an expression of how much she loved. Her tears actually were part of the beauty that they loved in her.

Sally's bag-lady fears did not end that day. It was rather the beginning of her journey as she learned—"with a little help from her friends"—that her sense of inadequacy did not reflect who she really was (she really was quite competent), and that her fears about herself were rooted not in her inadequacy but in the way she had locked away pieces of herself for fear that *they* (and not her) were unacceptable. Her covenant with herself to be perfect and polished (and thus hide all her rejected parts) had been an understandable defense against being seen by others as unacceptable. But her defense had left her feeling that she was unacceptable—a "bag lady"—rather than seeing (as she came to understand) that it was her family that had been unable to accept the fullness of her human- ity (tears included).

Sally's community held her into wholeness—supporting her as she re-membered herself, and offering her a message about herself different from the one she had come to expect. As she began to bring her sense of shame and inadequacy "to the light" of her group, she could see its origins, grieve all that she had lost, and eventually laugh at herself for the postures she had assumed to protect herself. Her bag-lady days—she later realized—were repetitions of the awful way she had felt when parts of herself (none of which were optional to her well-being) had been rejected, and she had been overwhelmed by her shame and loss and unable to find relief. Returning those feelings to the historical place of origin, she was freed of her worst fears and able to accept the vicissitudes of life—and the feelings she had about them—not as a reflection of her own inadequacies but as a part of the human condition.

Shame can be healed. But it takes the community of at least one other person (who is not going to reenact our original refusal) and the courage to walk through the valley of shame and grief. Theo- logically, we might say that new life (healing from the dance of shame) comes through the way of the cross—not because crosses are particularly holy, but because life is strewn with them and when we don't face them, we risk our own destruction.

Shame and Sin?

While we shall keep our reflections on brokenheartedness and sin for the final chapter in this section, we can appropriately stop for a moment and ponder what relationship shame might have to sin. Are we talking about two different phenomena? Or do they over- lap in some ways? Four observations come immediately to mind.

First, both sin as we have described it and shame as we have explored it in this chapter are expressed in postures of defense and refusal. In sin we structure for ourselves ways of being that can se- cure us against the pulling and tearing of life—structures that often violate others and our environment as well as ourselves. Similarly, the dance of shame is also a structure of self-securing as we seek through our dancing to protect ourselves from further painful experiences of shame. These dances are damaging to ourselves and often to others—and in this sense, since they are expressed in violation, might be called sin. Sin and shame thus may look a lot alike. But sin as we have defined it and shame are not the same, in that we have defined sin as a refusal, whereas shame is the result of being refused. They may look a lot alike as evidenced in human lives but claim different places of origin.

Second, if sin and shame may look alike (to the naked eye!), then it is possible that what the tradition has looked at as if it were sin may in fact at times not have been sin but shame. Thus, when some people confess their unworthiness before God, they may need not forgiveness (or not only forgiveness—since they may well need forgiveness for their acts or postures of violation) but healing from the shame that binds them.[12]

Third, if what we sometimes call sinful postures of refusal are dances of shame rooted in an original shaming rupture of our interpersonal bridge, then it is possible to understand how postures of refusal can be passed on from generation to generation. Whereas the classical (Augustinian) tradition has said that human beings inherit from one another a depravity (the inability not to sin), shame is passed on through our human vulnerability to being refused and through actual ruptures of the interpersonal bridge—ruptures that are not then healed. The dance of shame, while acted out at times in depraved ways, is actually born of deprivation.

Fourth, if the dance of shame appears to be an inherited fact (as one generation does in fact seem to pass on to the next postures of refusal that can be acted out in depraved ways), and if it can feel inherent to our being (we *are* shameful/depraved), then it is an inheritance originating in a historical event. The posture of refusal that is shame is not passed on in a depravity that is inherent to our being (as a depraved gene, perhaps), but is evoked as generation after generation (as well as institutionalized shaming systems) perpetuate patterns of shaming in acts of violation or refusal against one another. The fact that these refusals can occur at such an early age that their origin is buried in the unconscious, thus creating the feeling that we are shameful (depraved), could then explain theologians' sense that our sin (postures of refusal—some, perhaps, rooted in shame) is born in us and is inherent to our being. However, where what appears to be sin is actually born of shame, then postures of refusal are not inevitable to the human being—dances of shame can be avoided if ruptures in the relational bridge are attended to—nor are they inherent to our being, although our innate relationality and accompanying vulnerability (as well as the way in which we both

accidentally and intentionally miss each other) do make both violation and compensating dances of shame highly probable.

---

[1] Jill Ker Conway, *The Road from Coorain* (New York: Knopf, 1989), p. 66.

[2] "Panoptical" here refers to Jeremy Bentham's "Panoptican," a prison where
the prisoners were watched at all times. (It is referred to by Elizabeth A. Clark.
See the following note for bibliographical reference.)

[3] Elizabeth Clark, "Sex, Shame, and Rhetoric: En-Gendering Early Christian
Ethics," *JAAR* (Summer 1991), Vol. LIX, No. 2 , pp. 221–246. The church's teaching on sexuality and selfishness can be seen as two examples of how shaming is
used as a form of control.

[4] Because our first concern in being shamed is to hide, evidence of these overt
abuses is often hidden beneath a veneer of normalcy. One battered wife, for
instance, went to church each week hiding her bruises under her dresses. It was
only after her husband finally beat her to death that the woman's pastor realized the woman had always worn long-sleeved dresses to church—unusual at-
tire for a woman in the Southwest. In this case, the dress was a way of hiding
and a scream for help at the same time.

[5] Gershen Kaufman, *Shame: The Power of Caring* (Rochester, Vt.: Schenkman
Books, Inc., 1992), p. vii. Kaufman's work has been the most informative source
on shame for the purposes of this chapter—especially since he focuses on the
rupture of the relational bridge as the source of shame. Other valuable resources
on shame are listed in the bibliography at the end of his book.

[6] John Bradshaw makes this point in his description of good shame in *Healing
the Shame That Binds You* (Deerfield Beach, Fla.: Health Communications, Inc.,
1988).

[7] Ibid., p. 9.

[8] The theory of broken bridges, patterns of internalization, and defensive
maneuvers covered in this section are discussed in Kaufman, *Shame: The Power
of Caring*, Part I.

[9] Ibid., pp. 79–98.

[10] There are several possible meanings for perfection. Most commonplace is
the sense of being "without flaw." In the Sermon on the Mount, where Jesus tells
his followers to be "perfect," he is using the word to mean "complete": fulfilling
their *teleos*. This second meaning is not the problematic one to which I refer in
this chapter.

[11] Kaufman, *Shame: The Power of Caring*, pp. 133–178.

[12] See Laurel Arthur Burton's article, "Original Sin or Original Shame," Quar-
terly Review, (Winter 1988-89), pp. 31–41 for such an argument. Also, see Don
Capps's *The Depleted Self: Sin in a Narcissistic Age* (Minneapolis: Fortress Press,
1993) and his articles on Augustine (referenced in note 19 of chap. 3, p. 44),
where he argues that Augustine was shamed as a youth and what he later spoke
of as his sin is more a reflection of his sense of depravity, born of his shame.

Chapter 5

The Dance of the Generations

In those days they shall no longer say:
"The parents have eaten sour grapes, .
and the children's teeth are set on edge."
But all shall die for their own sins; the teeth of everyone who
eats sour grapes shall be set on edge.

—Jeremiah 31:29–30

The dance of alienation that is the dance of the generations is often scripted beneath the lines of our ordinary daily lives. It is as common as a constant need to look in a loved one's face to see if "everything is all right." It is as familiar as the mild sense of dread that creeps in around extended family reunions. It is reflected in the moments of self-doubt we feel every time someone else makes a career choice. Our kids see it in our faces when we try to hide from them our disappointment. It is a subtext hidden beneath most of the decisions we make in life.

Karen had worked long and thoughtfully on the plans for her ordination service. She had chosen hymns that reminded her of the community that had nurtured her through her advanced training. She had invited an old friend to preach the sermon. She had found two members of the church she had served as a young seminarian to pray for her. She had even convinced her oldest daughter to read the scripture lessons. She had tried to have the service represent all the different pieces of her life.

The one "piece" of her life, though, that Karen had not known how to integrate into her service was her parents. They were both only nominal Christians who hadn't shown a great deal of interest in church. More important, they had never shown a lot of enthusiasm for her decision to prepare herself for ministry. Still, she told herself, they *had* elected to drive across the country to attend the service; they must feel some sense of celebration for her accomplishment. So she had decided that, at the end of the service, she would include them in her acknowledgment of those who had supported her.

On the day of the big service, Karen's house was in an uproar. Each of her four children wanted help in dressing for the occasion; her husband had called to say he would have to work overtime and would meet them at the church; trays of food sent by friends filled the kitchen for the late-night gathering she had planned. In the midst of this, her parents arrived to drive them to the church. So focused was Karen on the service to come that she was completely taken off guard when she walked down the stairs to greet her parents and found her mother standing in the middle of the chaotic living room, shaking her head, while she clucked her tongue and said to the children: "Your mother never really was much of a housekeeper anyway."

What, Karen thought, did her mother mean by that statement? Surely Karen wasn't the only one who lived in this house and bore responsibility for its unkempt state. Surely the event of this day justified a bit of chaos. Besides, their house had always been neat enough. Her mother's comment, she decided, was unfair and she dismissed it as that.

But the more she thought about her mother, the angrier she became. Her mother's comment had been very unsupportive of her, even undermining. On the eve of her big day, her mother had pricked a hole in her ordination balloon. Was Karen really inadequate as a housekeeper, she asked herself? (Did she even think of herself as a housekeeper? Was that a part of the problem?) Was her mother proud of her accomplishments—earning both a divinity and an advanced ministerial degree while co-parenting four children (and not going crazy)? Or did her mother's comment reflect an ambivalence about Karen and all the talents that Karen had struggled all these years to identify and develop (and a disappointment that Karen was not more like her)?

The more she thought, the more Karen realized that her mother's comment had not been the first of its kind. Rather, Karen remembered, throughout Karen's whole life her mother had repeatedly expressed ambivalence about her. She had counseled Karen as a child to "tone down" her energies in school. When Karen had preached a sermon on Youth Sunday at her local church, her mother's only comment had been that she should have spoken more loudly. When Karen had decided to change her major in college from education (her mother had been a teacher when she was a young woman), her mother protested that she would never get a job. And when Karen decided in midlife to attend seminary, her mother's first question had been, "But what about the children, dear?"

Although Karen had always been aware of these pieces of her relationship with her mother, she had never strung them together in this way. As a result, she felt stung by what she had to acknowledge was at least her mother's ambivalence and at most her mother's corrosive lack of support for her (especially corrosive because it often came wrapped in a blanket of care and concern) as she had sought to live the most complete life she could fashion for herself.

But her thoughts didn't remain with her mother. Karen started to remember her own ambivalence about most of the decisions she had made for herself in her adult life. The decision to go to seminary had tied her in knots for years as she struggled with guilt over not being home full-time with her kids. As she had prepared to write her dissertation, she had harbored a fear that the process would probably kill her. In fact, as she had looked for the right room to set up as her office, she often had imagined herself lying on a couch or bed in the room feeling life drain out of her. (The reality was just the opposite, however. Upon earning her degree, Karen had a physical and was told by her physician that she had never been in better health!) Even as she now took on the task of ministry (with the full support of her husband), she worried about whether she could be "enough" for the people of her new congregation.

As Karen put together the pieces of her own ambivalence with the fact of her obvious abilities and accomplishments, she wondered how she had ever learned to doubt herself so routinely. Seeing clearly how deeply her self-doubt was rooted in her very being (there was nothing superficial about her struggle), Karen began to suspect that she had—somewhere along the route of her childhood—learned to make her mother's ambivalence about herself her own. Her own doubts and fears were a reflection of the doubts and fears of the woman who had nurtured her. They had become an almost invisible piece of herself, a dominant text with which she had struggled as she had sculpted her life.

Karen was sobered by this revelation. But she was also hopeful that her professional development and the style of marriage relationship she and her husband had shaped showed that she was able to break the hold of the mirror-imaging that had undermined her sense of herself. Karen decided, then, to return to her mother's house (taking her briefcase with her, to remind herself who she was in case she managed to forget) and confront her mother about her lack of support. It would be nice, she thought, to have her mother look at her and see her real face (assuming that she could keep her real face when her mother looked at her) and to have her acknowledge Karen in all her strength and vulnerability without needing to undermine what she saw. Although Karen knew this probably was unlikely, she decided to tuck the image in her briefcase anyway. She might need it sometime.

The thought that mothers and daughters identify with one another is not a new realization. Daughters need to identify with their mothers as a part of practicing who they are to be. When my daughter Kathryn was five, I asked her over breakfast one morning what she wanted to be when she grew up. She answered quickly, "I want to be a mommy." I thought about that response for a moment, and then in curiosity I asked her, "And what do mommies do?" "Oh," she answered, "they teach at Pittsburgh Theological Seminary!" This was an appropriate (if also amusing) response for her at her age (the desire to be like her mother), just as her adolescent resistance to anything that resembles me is also appropriate. My job in Kathryn's imaging of herself is simply to receive her image and marvel as she tries it on for herself (What a good mommy you will be! The world needs good scientists!).

The identification that Karen had with her mother, however, was not this playful dance of coming to know herself. Karen had not been liberated by her identification with her mother to construct her best way of being in the world. Rather, she had been crippled. She had come to internalize her mother's fears and ambivalence (as well as her mother's expectation that Karen should imitate her) at her own expense. If my task as a parent is to accept my children, marvel at them, and reflect back to them my support for the ways of being themselves that they reveal to me (and if we can assume that this is the task of any parent), then Karen and her mother had reversed the imaging process. Rather than feeling her mother's support for her efforts reflected back to her, Karen had felt the vacuum of her mother's ambivalence return to her. Seeing herself mirrored in this way, she had learned ambivalence and self-doubt as part of who she was. She thus had come to reflect her mother rather than to become herself.

Psychologists[1] tell us that relationships are central to human development. Not only are they crucial in our need for others to nurture us as we grow, but the relationships that sustain (or fail to sustain) us are the "stuff" out of which we build ourselves. We learn who we are as human beings by watching other human beings; we learn how to treat others by watching how others treat each other (and by watching their response to how we treat them); we learn how to treat ourselves by how others treat us. These bundles of relationships become the resources out of which we construct ourselves. (And we do not have to limit these bundles of relationships to the human realm. We also have relationships with animals, with the natural environment, with loved "objects.")

We also learn who we are by watching how others respond to us. If they receive us with delight, we learn that we are delightful. If they look at us with concern, we learn that something might be the matter. If they mirror our joy or sorrow back to us, we learn that we have joys and sorrows and that they are acceptable. If they look at us in horror or rejection, we learn that we (or those parts of ourselves) are rejectable. (We also learn whether we can tolerate horror and rejection on the faces of our caregivers.)

My grandson, Stephen, comes to visit me and we begin a game of recognition with one another. I look on his face with absolute delight, and he looks back at me—for just a moment, then turns his head away almost as if my gaze is more than he can stand. But then he looks at me again (to see if I'm still here?), and I return his look with great pleasure. "Yes, you are here," I am telling him, "and I think that you are wonderful!" Again he looks away—but this time with a smile and an actual shudder of delight.

This short game with my infant grandson is a dance of welcome and delight. Taking but a few moments, it may seem just a trivial passing. But it is important. Seeing me respond to him, seeing my delight, Stephen knows that he is acceptable. What great joy at being (and at being related) fills his little soul.

This dance of welcome and delight is only one of a remarkable repertoire of dances Stephen will develop with his mom and dad and the rest of his receiving community (which includes his aunts, uncles, grandparents as well as friends, teachers, ministers, pediatricians, etc.) as he grows up. In these dances, he will reveal the whole range of human needs and emotions; and his ability to incorporate all these needs and emotions into his becoming self will depend on the way his community receives them (and him) and mirrors them back to him. Stephen's community will not have to be perfect for him to be able to grow to his fullest possibility; it will need only to be "good enough."[2]

Not everyone, of course, receives good enough parenting. Sometimes parents are so preoccupied with other things in their lives that they do not notice what is going on in their child's life, presenting their child not eyes that delight, but a gaze that seems not to see at all.[3] Sometimes parents take out on their children the "that's life" quality of their own lives —blaming their child's behavior for what has happened to them. When this happens, a child can learn to "put away" those awful "things." ("Billy, if you just weren't so clingy I'd be able to get my work done!") Sometimes parents—who in their own childhood learned to "put away" some parts of themselves— are unable to tolerate the same parts in their own children, teaching their children also to hide them out of sight. (Karen's mother might fit into this category.) Sometimes parents can even replicate their own parents' refusals while intending to do just the opposite. (When I was an adolescent, I was told I could not pierce my ears—couldn't express myself in that way. I vowed not to do the same thing to my daughter. So, when she was ten, I gave her the gift of pierced ears. When she was fifteen, however, and wanted a second piercing—to express herself in her own way—I let her know that I was repulsed by the idea, just as my father had been by my entreaty.) To fail to find ourselves in glazed-over eyes, to be met not with approval and delight but horror and rejection, is to know refusal—the emptiness of a vacuum where welcoming arms should be. For many children, that refusal evokes a fear of abandonment that is intolerable. So they do whatever they feel is needed to make sure that they survive (that the eyes that look on them do so with interest and delight)—to make sure they are not abandoned again.

Sarah was only seven, but she had trouble falling asleep at night. Alone in her bed, she would rehearse all the worries of the day and project them into the night. She was afraid that her house would catch fire and burn down or that her baby sister would fall into a puddle and drown. (She also worried over how she would save her family if all these things did happen!) When her fears became unbearable, Sarah would creep down the stairs to the living room where her parents sat reading in the safe, warm light. She would quietly whimper, "I can't sleep." When she was impatiently asked why she couldn't sleep, she haltingly would tell her parents of her fears. Turning back to their reading (and this happened for many nights), her parents would tell her that the house wouldn't burn down and that babies don't drown in mud puddles (not attending to her fears and the fact that houses do burn down, and that sometimes babies do drown in bathtubs!) and send her back to bed. Not wanting to disobey her parents or arouse their anger, Sarah would then return to her bedroom (having learned not to share her fears with her parents), curl up into a tight ball, and cry herself to sleep. Later on as an adult, as she prepared herself for bed, Sarah would still be plagued with fears that were matched with a foreboding sense of her aloneness.

The tragedy of the child's situation of abandonment is often compounded because the child does not yet have the ability to understand adequately what is going on in her family (to know all the possible reasons for her parents' behavior) and has not yet developed a wide repertoire of responses that she can call upon to cope with that situation. What she knows most deeply is that if she does not have the love of her parents—if her parents are consumed by grief or worry, by disappointment or anger that keep them from gazing in delight at their child—then the child is at risk.

The courage of children in this situation is amazing. Confronting a condition (their parents' behavior) over which they have no control (the illusion of childhood is that in fact we are very powerful)—and often unaware of the other factors that might affect the parents' behavior (e.g., the state of their marriage; their relationships at work; serious financial problems; the inability to deal with their own feelings, having been poorly parented themselves; alcoholism; physical or mental illness; etc.)—children begin making adjustments in their own behavior (putting away rejected pieces of themselves, taking on new responsibilities) in the hope that their parents' sadness will be resolved or their interest will be caught and they will once again bless their child with eyes that see and bring life. In fear of abandonment, then, they abandon their own developmental dance (which they could not make without a partner anyway). Ironically, out of wanting desperately to be seen and mirrored, children learn how to read their parents' faces—not to reflect back to them who they (the children) are, but to see if they are pleased. The task of knowing ourselves becomes derailed in the dance of giving to others what we think they want so that they will love us. In a grotesque reversal, the child's love is poured out that the parent might live. This reversal, this dance of the generations, is what psychologist Alice Miller has called the drama of the gifted child.[4]

A vivid picture of one such reversal is revealed to us in D. H. Lawrence's short story "The Rocking Horse Winner." As the story begins we read:

> There was a woman who was beautiful, who started with all the advantages, yet she had no luck. She married for love, and the love turned to dust. She had bonny children, yet she felt they had been thrust upon her, and she could not love them. They looked at her coldly, as if they were finding fault with her. And hurriedly she felt she must cover up some fault in herself. Yet what it was that she must cover up she never knew. Nevertheless, when her children were present, she always felt the centre of her heart go hard. This troubled her and in her manner she was all the more gentle and anxious for her children, as if she loved them very much. Only she herself knew that at the centre of her heart was a hard little place that could not feel love, no, not for anybody. Everybody else said of her: "She is such a good mother. She adores her children." Only she herself, and her children themselves, knew it was not so. They read it in each other's eyes.[5]

There were three children in this family, a boy and two little girls. They had a pleasant enough house, servants, a garden. However:

> Although they lived in style, they felt always an anxiety in the house. There was never enough money. And so the house came to be haunted by the unspoken phrase: There must be more money! There must be more money! The children could hear it all the time, though nobody said it aloud. They heard it at Christmas, when the expensive and splendid toys filled the nursery. Behind the shining modern rocking-horse, a voice would start whispering: There must be more money! There must be more money! And the children would stop playing to listen for a moment. They would look into each other's eyes, to see if they had all heard. There must be more money! There must be more money.[6]

Paul, the son in this story, is a "gifted child." Born into a family that ostensibly loved him, Paul soon discerned on his mother's face the hardness in the center of her heart that made it impossible for her to love either him or his sisters. Behind the gestures of love—the toys, his new rocking horse—Paul could sense that all was not well. And so he listened to the family myth that said that what was not well was the family's lack of money. This myth seemed to echo in the halls of their home: "There must be more money." And Paul, knowing that he needed his mother's love most of all in order to survive, decided to solve the problem. If there was no money, then he would find some (reflecting his understanding that if he found the money, then everything would be okay and his mother would be able to love him).

By riding himself into a trance on the back of his new rocking horse, Paul discovered that he was able to discern the name of the horse that would win the next day's horse race. Secretly (with the help of the gardener) placing bets on that horse, Paul was able to win money, which he then arranged to be given anonymously to his mother so that she would have enough money. Only Paul's plan did not work out as he expected. (A gifted child's plans rarely do. Or, if they seem to be successful, it is at the great expense of constant surveillance and maintenance.) Rather, the money Paul earned was never enough. The halls still echoed; the look in his mother's eyes never changed (because, of course, the hardness in her heart never was about money). Finally, in an attempt surely to make enough money in the big race to come Paul rode himself into a state of exhaustion from which he never recovered. Trying to make his mother happy (and thereby, he assumed, winning for himself her undying affection), seeking to win for himself what should have been his birthright (his mother's love), hoping to elude an abandonment that had already happened, Paul abandoned his own childhood need to be taken care of in order to take care of his mother. Needing to be parented, Paul instead assumed a parental role. No longer just a little boy, he died—sacrificed on the altar of his mother's hardened heart.[7]

This story raises several questions for us about the dance of the generations. Why does no one see what Paul is doing and stop him? Where is Paul's father? Why is Paul's mother unable to love her children? Where did the hardness in her heart come from? Whose face was it that looked upon her coldly, "as if they were finding a fault": her children's (who would look on her face with great hope and would find no comfort in her faults), or an older, more ancient face that had not been able to look on her with the love and acceptance she needed in her youth? Why is it that no one but her children is able to see that her love is a charade? And why does Paul ride himself to death for a love that is not there to win?

Paul's story—while quite unusual—is also the familiar story of how many children, fearing the loss of their parents' love, make understandable assumptions about what is going on in their parents' hearts and take enormously damaging responsibility for making things right. That children abandon themselves in order to survive makes sense. But this story is also the story of Paul's mother. Written between the author's lines we can find clues to her story—for she is also a gifted child. We can see, for instance, in the critical looks she believes she sees on the faces of her children a fault-finding eye that probably told her from an early age that she was not acceptable. (It is a part of the drama of gifted children that the fault-finding eye becomes internalized as their own and is then projected onto others, so that they will see reflected even on their children's faces the rejection they saw in the eyes of their parents.) Is it any wonder that she, who knew herself as rejectable and thus never got the chance to complete the tasks of her own childhood, felt as if her own children had been "thrust upon" her—demanding a love she had not received and had trouble giving? (And is it likely that she had hoped to find in her children's faces the love that she had never been able to win—and that she might have felt depleted when she realized that her children needed her to love them?) Where did she learn that she couldn't love? (Did no one receive the love she must have offered?) Could it be that her "hard heart" was really hardened by the scar tissue of her own broken heart?

This story, ostensibly about Paul, the "rocking horse winner," is also about a cycle of brokenheartedness—where a mother's inherited dance of self-rejection (there was always a fault to find!) is reflected in everyone's eyes. She is rejected (by a mother who herself was rejected?) and sees that rejection reflected back to her in the eyes of her children. They see her rejection of herself reflected toward them in her eyes that look to them for approval but see only fault-finding and rejection. Her rejection is not of the children (in fact, her furious activity to appear to be a loving mother reflects her desire to compensate for her hardness of heart and to love them as best she can). Rather, she is acting out of her own learned rejection of herself. But, in doing so, in her preoccupation with her own rejection (her awareness of the hardening of her heart, the fault-finding eye she saw even on her children's faces), she reenacts upon her children the very rejection she has suffered. The children see that rejection on her face and assume it is rejection of themselves (and they confirm their own sense of rejection in each other's eyes). Paul's intent to win his mother's love reflects his own brokenheartedness (his mother doesn't love him), his fear that he might be unlovable (a child is too young to assume that he receives no love because the parent can't love), and his new (and incorrect) knowledge that love is something that must be earned.

In this story of "the rocking horse winner" who loses everything, we see how the dance of the generations is passed on from parent to child as each generation—in the dance of self-rejection and searching for a love never received—fails to give its children the love they need, thereby breaking their hearts as well. The dance of the generations is both between generations and within each individual, each internalizing the whole drama as if it were only his or her own. They are locked together in a dance of alienation born of refusal and a broken heart. Tragically, children are more than victims in this dance for they often, out of good hearts, participate in their own rejection.

Of course, mothers are not the only ones who can refuse their children and leave them brokenhearted. In both Karen's and Paul's stories, for instance, the fathers are absent. They have in their silence already abandoned their children. Silence, we learn, is not benign. Children fill it in with all sorts of messages.

But fathers can also actively form their children in brokenheartedness. The story of Bull McCabe (from the film *The Field*) is the story of how a father's drive to ensure his family's survival ultimately (and ironically) leads to the deaths of both his sons. This story reveals to us how the dance of the generations can be born not only out of direct refusals (such as Karen's) but out of a well-meant (and misplaced) commitment to the child's well-being that fails to consider what the child really wants and needs. In the name of love we see people not treated with the awe and respect owed to each person in his or her mysterious uniqueness, but instead chewed up by the cogs of the family wheel of fortune.

Bull McCabe was the oldest son in his family. He was born and raised during the potato famine that was decimating Ireland. (Sometimes, we will see, adversity enhances the dance of the generations and grants it legitimacy. We must, after all, survive.) His family's one possession of value was an emerald-green field dug out from the surrounding rocky hills. The field, Bull was told, was a treasure. (It was the key to the family's survival.) But it was a treasure that had be tended faithfully.

The truth was that the field never really had offered the family survival at all. In fact, the viewer of the film realizes, it had produced only enough to support one child at a time. But this was the family myth (a myth like Paul's) and it held for Bull a promise: the promise of his father's love. So it was that Bull, in loyalty to his father's myth of the field, failed to see the lie of it when all his other brothers and sisters left home because there was no way to support them. (He instead took their leaving as an act of disloyalty.) Nor did he let himself see how his loyalty to the field denied his mother her final comfort. (He chose to finish tending the field rather than fetching the priest who would have administered to her the last rites. Actually, Bull did realize that his decision had hurt his mother but was proud of what he had done because he believed that he had seen in his father's eyes when Bull had put the field first, not tears of grief over the passing of his wife, but tears of pride in Bull for his loyalty!) If he fulfilled the promise of the myth, he believed, his father would continue to look on him with pride. Thus, long after his father's death, Bull continued to see the field as the symbol of that pride and to insist that the family keep the field to keep that blessing.

Bull himself had two sons, who were also inheritors of the myth of the field. What both sons really wanted was their father's blessing. Instead, what they both received was their father's obsession with the field and his demand that they be as loyal as he had been. (This is the way to the father's love.) But their father's obsession was not life-giving to the sons. One hanged himself to make sure that his brother would inherit the field, while the other became cruel, reflecting the cruelty of his family system. (Bull, interestingly enough, saw this cruelty as a weakness in his *son* and not as a flaw in the family system.) This son tried desperately to please his father, but finally, after admitting to himself that the field had never been what he really wanted, he tried to leave home by running off with a tinker's daughter. This was the ultimate disloyalty, since tinkers have no land. Tragically, he was killed trying to help his father one last time before leaving home. Bull, deprived of the love (the bread of life) he had always sought from his father (instead he gave him a field of stones), demanded love from his sons (instead of giving it to them) in the form of extreme loyalty. In the end, there was no one left to bless.

The dance of the generations is tragic. One rejected and depleted generation passes on to the next generation more rejection and depletion. It is a dance of abandonment as those depleted of love struggle to gain the mirroring they never got (are you my mother?[8]) in the eyes of others (lovers, bosses, friends). They do so fearing and often finding once again on the face of the other the look of rejection they know so well (for they bring "maws"[9] hungrier than any relationship can fill). They do so fearing (in the face of repeated rejections) that the rejection faithfully reflects who they really are (or fearing—as in the case of Bull McCabe—that if they look hard enough at the myths of loyalty they have accepted instead of love, the myths will crumble, leaving them with only an empty promise). And they act out this rejection on the next generation.

Meanwhile, they have forgotten—or never had a chance to learn—the process whereby human beings freely reveal to another not what they think the other wants to see but what is genuinely theirs to share and have the pleasure of having that received with grace. They have learned not that love can be unconditional, but that it always has a price: On the one hand, love must be earned (so one loses the joy of spontaneous give-and-take) and on the other, loving means filling another's needs. Love, Daniel Day Williams has said, means to desire the freedom of the other.[10] In this dance of alienation, love is anything but liberating. It traps everyone in its snare. It becomes a dance of bondage. If trust is forged out of relationships where one is respectfully received (and one's love is also respectfully received instead of demanded or overlooked), then the dance of the generations undermines not only love and freedom but trust, both in self and in the other. One learns not to trust the other but to manipulate the other to give what one wants.

Healing the Dance

If the dance of alienation that is the dance of the generations is in fact often a subtext that governs our behavior and our relationships to others and to ourselves, and is almost invisible because it is so familiar (even if hated) and so painful to examine, then healing comes first of all from lifting it from subtext to the awareness of how formative it is in our lives.

Barbara was determined to give her daughter what she had never received as a child. This was a valid intent. But Barbara became so obsessed with giving Kelly what she herself hadn't received that she was totally unaware that she had become so focused on her own behavior (Was she being a good enough mother?) that she was totally missing what her daughter was asking for (thereby repeating her own mother's self-preoccupation).

One day, however, Kelly exploded at her mother. "You don't really care about me at all," she said. "All you care about is yourself and your perfect family dynamics." Seeing the rage in her daughter's eyes (and recognizing in that rage remnants of her own rage at her mother), Barbara was caught up short. Had she, she wondered, despite her best efforts, ended up playing out her own childhood rejection with her daughter? How in the world had she let such a thing happen?

If the dance of the generations is alienation that is passed on between the generations, then healing comes not only by seeing through to the invisible text of our lives, but also by breaking the cycle of alienation. If each generation is not given the love and respect it needs from the previous generation and seeks to find its recompense on the faces of the next generation, then healing can come when, instead of refusing our children, we refuse the process. And to refuse the process, we must be more aware of what the process is than Barbara initially was. But this refusal is not without its costs.

Richard had not had much of an adolescence. He had never felt sure enough of his parents' love to risk a real rebellion. When his parents said they didn't want him to dance, he never learned to dance. When they said they wanted him home, he dropped out of a geology club because he wouldn't be able to go on their field trips. When they wanted him to be talented and witty, he willingly obliged. Even though Richard learned how to reap the rewards of his family's system, he did not feel happy. He did not know how to relate to other kids, and a genuine loneliness gnawed at him inside.

When Richard had children he vowed (like Barbara) that they would be allowed to be "real" teenagers. This didn't come easily to him. It was only one day when he lost his temper with his son because his son talked back to him that he realized he was on the brink of demanding of his son the absolute loyalty his father had demanded of him. He tried to support his children in all their interests—listening carefully to what they said or felt and faithfully and enthusiastically mirroring to them what he saw. He "understood" when they didn't want to sit with the family at social outings. He tolerated the occasional times when they would come in later than curfew (always, he noted, with an outlandish but barely reasonable explanation). He wanted them to be free to break away and know that he would pay attention, be patient, and watch them through it.

Richard believed that what he was doing for his children was the right thing—freeing them from the cycle that his family had ingrained in him. And he was right. What Richard hadn't bargained for, though, was the great grief he would suffer during the process. The freer Richard's children were to experience the full gamut of teenage emotions, the more Richard found himself grieving the fact that he hadn't been free to feel those same emotions when he was a teenager. When they spoke up to him and challenged his beliefs, he was both proud of them and empty inside in memory of the times when he had swallowed what he had wanted to say back to his parents. Richard came to realize that healing the dance of the genera-tions meant not only stopping the cycle of rejection, but also healing the emptiness within himself.

As we see, then, in Richard's case, healing comes not only through stopping the cycle of the generations but also (our third point) through the companion process of grieving. If grief is a part of the human process whereby we heal from the death of a loved one, then it is also a process where we can heal from the losses of our childhood. If the dance of the generations is one in which chil-dren, never seeing in their parents' eyes the acceptance that is cru-cial to their well-being, abandon themselves in order to win that look from their parents (or seek desperately to find it in the eyes of another), then healing comes when they see through their dance of abandonment to its root in the lack of affirmation and grieve that loss. A child is too alone to tolerate this grief (and thereby learns to become gifted); it is to be hoped that as adults they can both tolerate the pain and find someone to share it with.[11]

As Nicodemus reminded Jesus, we cannot climb back into our mother's womb and start the process over again. Whereas we now realize that child-parent relationships are more mutual than we had once realized (babies are not just passive receivers—they also give), the time of childhood is a time to be selfish, to be the cen-ter of the universe, to have all one's needs for affirmation and comfort met. Once that time is lost, it is a major loss, and part of the process of healing is accepting this reality (accepting, for in-stance, that one's spouse cannot be one's mother/father) and liv-ing with its injustice.

Loss is not the final word, however. Since we can never find another mother or father, we can learn that the ones we had—though limited—probably did love us. (Karen's mother both undermined and loved as best she could; Bull's promise of the field was the best blessing he knew how to give.) We can also learn to piece together a community of "good enough" loving to support us. We can find friends, lovers, therapists, and teachers who, when not compelled to replace a love that is lost, can still love (and receive our love) enough to heal our hearts. These relationships then can become the new bundles of relationships that we use to weave into a patch that can begin to fill up the hole inside.

Finally, if the dance of the generations is not only about the loss of a parent's love, but also about the loss of parts of ourselves that were rejected (or squelched as we learned to doubt them or to patch other people's dreams over them), then healing means recovering the lost feelings, talents, dreams, and possibilities and integrating them into ourselves as well. This is also best facilitated by a "receiving community" who can hear us into dreams long forgotten, and hold feelings and talents that have been kept out of sight.[12]

And Sin?

Again, in this dance of the generations we see a dance of alienation that is formed not out of a refusal but out of an experience of being refused, an experience of brokenheartedness. Born out of a need to survive and the incredible ignorance of childhood, we learn all sorts of dances to protect ourselves and earn or keep the love we need to have. That dance effectively becomes a posture of refusal (hiding all that has been put away) that we then perpetuate upon our children (or others who are vulnerable as we were when we were refused).

Five points here seem crucial in our discussion of brokenheartedness and sin. First, the dance of the generations reveals to us how alienation can in fact be inherited from one generation to another. Situations of rejection breed dances of alienation and more situations of rejection. While this rejection is inherited by being actively rejected, it is also tragically communicated because one who should love cannot love but greets us with a vacuum rather than an embrace.

Second, while this dance of the generations can be communicated through overt acts of rejection, it is also communicated as the rejected one *surmises* that he or she is rejected (as in the case of Paul), when the other's behavior may have more to do with his or her own dance of rejection than with the need to reject us. We, then, participate in our own rejection both as we internalize the ways others actually do reject us and as we surmise that we are rejectable and continue to act in self-rejecting ways. Moreover, we perpetuate the dance of the generations as we act out that self-rejection on others.

Third, if sin is a state of idolatry—the desire to secure oneself by grasping something which by definition cannot secure one—the dance of the generations is one that breeds idolatry. If "good enough" parenting can teach us to love with an open hand (love is plentiful enough that we need not grasp it as if it will disappear at any moment) and to accept inevitable losses as a piece of life, then the dance of the generations leaves us painfully aware of our vulnerability and with the longing for security greatly intensified.[13] Out of fear of abandonment, one turns those who should be fleeting gods in our evolving pantheon (our parents) into idols that govern our lives. And the very act of loving is transformed into a compulsive and idolatrous dance.

Fourth, if the dance of the generations turns love into compulsion, robbing it of its spontaneity and freedom, and if children never get to experience a love that truly is for their own well-being (and to develop trust that others can love them in this way) but must always be looking over their shoulders to see if their parents are "still there," then the dance of the generations is an act of continual violation that is sin. The possibility of the new generation is sacrificed for the broken heart of the previous one.

Finally, if sin creates suffering (the dance of the generations), then the redemption of that sin is not without its costs. To end the cycle of this dance of the generations, someone must stop perpetuating the violence, and this entails even more suffering. But only then will the parents' sour grapes no longer be perpetrated on their children.

---

[1] For example, see Jessica Benjamin, *The Bonds of Love* (New York: Pantheon Books, 1988). See also her bibliography and extensive end notes. This insight into the centrality of relationships to who we are is also foundational to theologians and philosophers of the school of process thought.

[2] D. W. Winnicott is responsible for the term "good enough" mothering to describe this process. See *The Maturational Processes and the Facilitating Environment: Studies in the Theory of Emotional Development* (New York: International Universities Press, 1965). Carroll Saussy, in *God Images and Self-Esteem*, is responsible for the term "good enough parenting."

[3] This preoccupation often is not intentional on the part of the parents. Sometimes life is hard and parents are depleted and justifiably preoccupied. Sometimes parents and children are temperamentally mismatched, or babies are colicky, which makes for extra stress on parents.

[4] Alice Miller, *The Drama of the Gifted Child*, trans. by Ruth Ward (USA: Basic Books, 1981). This book has been very successful in this country—witnessed by its several editions. What Miller means by "gifted" in this title is not necessarily artistic or talented—although the gifted child may be these things. She means that the child must work very hard to earn his or her parents' love.

[5] D.H. Lawrence, "The Rocking Horse Winner," found in *The Critical Reader*, Roy Lamson, Hallett Smith, Hugh M. Maclean, Wallace W. Douglas, eds. (New York: W.W. Norton & Co., 1962), p. 525.

[6] Ibid., p. 525f.

[7] This insight into Lawrence's story was first made clear to me in "Hidden Secrets of Childhood" by Suzanne Short in *Psychological Perspectives*, pp. 100–117.

[8] See P.D. Eastman, *Are You My Mother?* (New York: Random House, 1960).

[9] This is Ed Farley's image, which is a part of the dynamics of sin. See *Good and Evil*, p.133. I use it here as a symptom of brokenheartedness.

[10] See Daniel Day Williams, *The Spirit and the Forms of Love* (New York: Harper & Row, 1968).

[11] In earlier editions of *The Drama of the Gifted Child*, Miller emphasizes the importance of the therapeutic relationship. In her latest edition—perhaps in response to the self-help movement—she encourages readers to do this on their own.

[12] See Elizabeth O'Connor, *The Eighth Day of Creation* (Waco, Tex.: Word Books, 1971), for a series of exercises one church used to help people recover lost dreams and desires.

[13] Families also enhance idolatrous ways when they perpetuate myths that cover over the losses and create the sense that loyalty to the myth will keep us safe and win the love we need to survive.

Chapter 6

The Loss of Mystery:
The Dance Becomes a March

> *Every family is a naturally and unself-consciously religious place because every family is a place where day after day, year after year, a coherent and often undeviating disposition toward ultimate reality is being expressed. The beliefs, rules, values, ideals, prejudices, passions, promises, betrayals, terrors, demons, and angels that every family passes before and onto its children declare, finally, where we who belong to this family stand in relation to the awesome powers of the universe. How generous or unforgiving, gentle or terrible, just or capricious is the Life Force? What is required of us to be in good faith with our Maker? How dangerous or how exhilarating is it to be alive?*
>
> —Robert Kegan
> *In Over Our Heads*[1]

Life holds for each of us the possibility to dance. There are dances of joy, of grief, of wonder, of delight, of coming together, of leaving, and of coming apart. Underlying these dances is a certain mystery. We suffer grief and discover paradoxically that when we suffer through it, such a process of suffering can heal. We feel angry and learn, despite our fears that anger can tear apart the fabric of connection, that anger can be a clue to something gone amiss—an invitation to set things right.[2] Far from disrupting, anger can be the beginning of a new way of being together. We birth a child and see something of ourselves in her, but also something strange and new (where did that come from?); or discover moments when, despite her dependency on us, she also reaches out to give us something. (A smile of recognition? "I see you, too.") We allow our children to be the center of their own universes, to be selfish for a while and watch as they grow into adults capable of great compassion. We are told that work is the purpose of life and we aim for fruitfulness and then discover that work without play becomes deadly—that times of sabbath (of not producing) are crucial to the process of creation. We feel at times that we have failed, only to wake up the next day and discover that what we thought was a failure was really the clue to a new beginning. When confronted with the awesome majesty of natural wonders, we can discover our terrifying smallness in relation to the universe, and yet feel strangely comforted. We can walk into a room feeling painfully self-conscious and be so drawn into the community or event that we paradoxically forget ourselves and feel the fullness of ourselves at the same time. We can feel as if we are no one but experience, in the presence of a listening ear, our very selves unfolding.

We are also daily confronted with others who are strangers to us, whose comings and goings are beyond our control, who come to us with their own centers of being that seem to threaten our constructed worlds. And we find despite the "otherness" that threatens us that the reality of the other's strangeness can mean also the good news that we are not alone on this planet, that there is the possibility for companionship (that someone might actually receive us with grace and delight)—an invitation to a dance of intimacy that can be more enjoyable than it is frightening. (And, if we are fortunate, even those we love and know best are still mysterious to us—always more than the sum of the many parts we have memorized.) Life has a mysterious, dancing cast. This is part of its beauty. This is also part of what we can find so frightening. Do we dare to trust that the feelings of grief, for instance, that threaten to overwhelm us will really bring us back to a healthy balance again? Can we believe that our anger can be other than destructive? Can we tolerate relationships where the ones we love are free to come and go and be okay in their strangeness to us?

This summer, my nineteen-year-old son decided to move out and get his own apartment. This has been a big step for both of us—as I weather another stage in the empty-nest syndrome and he has the breath-catching experience of being "on his own." Although in many ways this move is an abrupt one (he has cleaned out his room and taken almost all of his belongings with him, leaving hardly a shred of evidence that he was here), it is also one for which we have been preparing for years—with all our comings and goings from each other. With each of these "practices" we learned both the pleasure and the scariness (which might be part of the pleasure) of the leaving and the finding again. As he leaves this time I am reminded again that he is not me—that he is his own unique person (and that I am as well).

We are mother and son, yet stranger and stranger, as well. Sometimes this hurts. The hardest part of parenting for me is when I am left with an empty space where a warm body used to reside. But the joy of it is the adventure of watching the mystery of who he is unfold and of marveling at the whole new facets of himself he now chooses to bring to our relationship. I hope that in the respectful loving I try to practice, he learns something of an open-handed approach to life: to love passionately but to hold with an open hand; to welcome familiarity and strangeness; to greet life and enjoy it but to also let it flow on—to let himself be empty from time to time.[3]

Sometimes life the way we are given it can erode our appreciation of the mystery of life—our ability to do more with the fluctuations of life than merely survive. This can be through no one's fault at all. When Alice was twelve months old, her mother died of cancer. This happened many decades before social workers regularly informed surviving parents about how children cope (or fail to cope) with such devastating losses. People just assumed that Alice was fine because she was so little—and because she seemed to be okay. But Alice was not fine; her mother's loss left a gaping hole in Alice's psychic side that did not go away but continued to overwhelm her—especially during times of transition or stress. As an adult, Alice could see people around her respond to life with great resiliency, while she braced herself against whatever life would bring.

Sometimes social and family systems can be so cruel that children have no choice but to hold on to survive (and defend themselves), learning coping patterns that become so entrenched that the possibility of an open dance with life becomes remote. Raymond was born into poverty. He was regularly beaten as a child; once his father even picked him up by the heels and banged his head against the frozen radiators in his family's small apartment. Life was hard, and everyone in the family learned to fend for themselves. When he was twelve, Raymond was sent by the courts (because of repeated truancy) to a group home where he was to be given structure and some "tough love" that might give him some new opportunities in life. But the situation was too new and different and threatening to him, and he continually ran away, preferring the tough life on the streets (where he was attuned to the constant danger and knew how to survive) to the relative safety of the group home (where he would have to learn new skills).

Sometimes the very ruttedness of everyday routine, the systems that relate to us as a number and not a name, can also erode life's mystery—confining our identity to what can be encoded on a computerized form and our lives to a ten-foot-ceilinged universe. We learn to manage our world (and be managed by it) but not to wonder at it. When I was in graduate school, I used to climb Mount Baldy in the San Gabriel Mountains periodically just to remind myself that there was more to life than all the hoops that confronted me. On top of the mountain, I was better able to see the small world I had constructed to manage all the possibilities and disappointments that were confronting me.[4]

Sometimes the very systems into which we are born can undermine the possibility of living (and dancing) in the face of mystery. Structuralized racism and patriarchal gender roles, for instance, treat individuals as stereotypes, ignoring or rejecting the mystery of the individual that does not fit the definition. Sometimes these systems can teach us rules to live by (the basis for the family "religion" Kegan talks about above) that erode our abilities to know and express our feelings, that refuse to allow us to talk about and resolve our problems (and gain proficiency and resiliency for living—since life is always full of problems and challenges), that fail to accept us as not only like our families, but also as strange and unique—that refuse, that is, to welcome the mystery that is life and that is also each of us. (My family would always cluck their tongues when any of the children would show an enthusiasm for something that was not clearly within the family project or trajectory.)

Sometimes instead of being the bedrock of the dance of intimacy (for which we know early parent-child relationships are the basis) wherein we come to trust the unfolding of relationships (relationships that preserve the strangeness of the other as well as the familiarity),[5] these systems can teach us to control or to be controlled. Sometimes these systems fail to value the strangeness that is us— the good news of the uniqueness we can bring to an old world but which would also, in its difference, mean change for the old way. They seek instead to have us "toe the line" and leave us with a confused sense of who we are. And when these systems become violent, they pare down life to the bare fact of survival. (The fact that some do survive these systems and even go on to thrive despite them could be seen, however, as a mystery in its own right!)

These systems effectively teach that life, including our own feelings and needs, is dangerous. Why else would the family need such order? These systems can squeeze the mystery out of life and leave us either dancing a dance of control that is more like an orchestrated march in time to the beating of the family drum, a choreographed procession than it is a spontaneous dance *in response to* life, or—if our response to these systems is not to master its orchestrated cadence— then a sluggish, and perhaps despairing, dragging of our feet.[6]

The film *Ordinary People* is about life in all its messiness and how resistance to that messiness and to the possibility of mystery that accompanies it turns the dance of life with all its pain into a choreographed march. It becomes a procession that gives the illusion of beauty and control, in some way mimicking the beauty of mystery, but which undermines any possibility within the family for spontaneity and intimacy (which might, after all, hurt), for the wonder of being seen and accepted, of coming to know and accept the self, and the paradoxical joy and beauty that life even in its pain can give.

Ordinary People begins with a serenity and order that tells the viewer that the lives of ordinary people are stable and under control. We start with a view of a placid Lake Michigan, walk through an autumn vista (interestingly, seeing no people), view a neighborhood of large and well-cared-for houses, pass a sturdy-looking church, and end outside an imposing, classically structured school—all of these structures representing institutions of stability in a society. Throughout this scene, we hear the steady, predictable, and thus soothing melody of Pachelbel's *Canon* and hear a choir singing the opening refrain: "In the silence of our souls, O Lord, we contemplate thy peace."

The ordinary family we meet also seems at first sight to reflect a sense of order and calm. Calvin Jarrett, the father, is a kind, well-meaning man, someone you can trust. Even though throughout the movie he is mildly plagued with a sense of something not quite in order, he is usually easily diverted from his musings and drawn good-naturedly into the work and play that fill upper-middle-class life. Beth, his wife (played to perfection by Mary Tyler Moore), is simply exquisite. She is beautiful, always stylishly dressed, never a hair out of place. Her home is attractively if coldly decorated—everything seems to have its right place and she is meticulous in keeping it perfect. She even, we are told, fired a maid for not dusting the living room the right way. Her days are filled with errands, meal planning, social outings, shopping, and the myriad details of running a large house.[7]

Beth is one focus of this film. But what we know of her, other than her order and perfection, we have to piece together around the edges of the film, splicing together a comment here with a look of surprise there. Perhaps, we might conjecture, that's the only place she deals with the disorderly stuff of life—on its edges. We can guess from her husband's comments that Beth has always been disciplined, beautiful, and perfect—with her feelings and her life neatly under control. We know that looking good even when she and her loved ones must have felt lousy is important to her; she works at keeping up family appearances. And we can guess, from the few moments we see her with her own parents, that Beth's choreographed way of living is a trait she learned from childhood, where she was probably raised in a home that lived by the same rules. (When feelings are expressed rather than controlled, when conflict is brewing, change the subject, fix a meal, get out of town.) This, of course, is conjecture, based on two scenes in the movie where Beth's controlling way of dealing with adversity seems, from her parents' reactions, to be an established norm. What we do know from the film is that Beth—despite the illusion of being under control—is really terrified of life and what it brings her. The training she has received and practices so well—training in making life beautiful and keeping it under control—does not prepare her to handle, let alone embrace, life in all its sorrows and mystery. Life is messy. That is a part of its mystery. But, as Calvin tells her, Beth cannot "handle messy."

But despite all of Beth's efforts, all is not "perfect" in the Jarrett household (and by implication, neither is life perfect in other ordinary households). In the midst of the family lies a family secret (it's not a secret, but it seems that way because no one talks about it) and a young son in turmoil whose distress threatens to disturb the surface calm and order of the family system. (In fact, he is one of the voices singing the opening composition by Pachelbel. But there is no silence in his soul and definitely no peace. Even in that steady and glorious music, it seems, is the seed of unrest.)

Conrad, the son, is obviously a tortured young man. He cannot sleep or eat, he does not seem to know how to relate to his classmates, and his relationships with his parents—particularly with his mother—seem strained to the breaking point. The source of Conrad's distress, we learn, is twofold: his older brother has died in a tragic boating accident for which he feels responsible; he has just returned from the hospital where he was taken following a suicide attempt. Life is messy—it has its tragedies and the Jarrett family has just had its share.

But as the film progresses, it becomes apparent that the source of Conrad's distress is not only the hard fact that his brother has died and that he was unable to save him, but also that he has had no place in his family system to deal with his feeling of sadness and guilt. Without an outlet for his feelings, he feels isolated and crazy—as if neither he nor his feelings belongs. He begins to fear that he is probably expendable in the family circle—or that his mother would rather have his brother Bucky back than to have him. (Bucky was the perfect son—the one who fulfilled the family promise; Conrad is the one who messes things up.)

In fact, Beth *has* been overwhelmed by the loss of her older son and by the threatened loss of Conrad in his attempted suicide. (She never forgave him for that, he says. For making such a mess. All that blood. She even had to throw out the towels and re-grout the bathroom floor.) In order to protect herself from her pain, she makes a rule for her family that they must get on with their lives and not dwell on what has happened. Because talk of Bucky's death rehearses her grief, her lack of control over life, and her inability to keep her children safe, Beth will not allow anyone to talk about it. (She's adept at changing the subject—at focusing on torn shirts and shopping for new ones rather than on broken hearts and trying to heal them.) She avoids any contact that might allow some intimate exchange between herself and her remaining son. ("Can I help you Mom?" Conrad asks as she prepares for dinner. "Why don't you go clean out your closet?" she answers.) She wants to travel, to get away from anything that would remind her. It is no wonder that Conrad feels expendable.

Conrad, however, is eventually unable to comply with the family rules, and that puts him and his mother at odds with each other. He does at first attempt to "get on with" his life. (But it is questionable whose life he is trying to live—his own, or some likeness of his brother's. And for whom—himself, or to fulfill the family's need?) He tries to cooperate with the family plan but isn't able to shake off his pain, confusion, guilt—he is unable to function as he has in the past. He no longer can connect with his friends; he cannot focus in school; he even quits the swimming team. And the family rules leave him nowhere to go with his suffering (except another suicide attempt?). His pain and vulnerability are more than Beth can bear, so she pushes him away. (And experiencing this, he feels his pain and vulnerability are larger than he can bear as well.) She continues to care for him in a distant sort of way but really doesn't seem to notice who he is—except when he fails a test or quits the team without telling her. Nor does Conrad get to see who his mother really is. There is only one moment in the film when he sees her pain—sees something other than the distant woman who runs an orderly household and dwells on appearances. One day when she is alone in the house, she enters Bucky's room—which hasn't been changed since his death—and sits there, just remembering him. When Conrad finds her there, she immediately jumps up, hides her feelings, and in a distracted way asks Conrad how school was today. The chance for open, honest exchange is lost.

Luckily, Conrad does make other connections in this film. He finds a psychiatrist who gives him a safe place to express his feelings and face his losses. (Conrad comes to Dr. Berger to learn how to be in control of himself—he is his mother's son in some ways. Berger, however, is not interested in control but in life, even when it is painful.) He meets and begins to date Janine—a vivacious, caring young woman who is prone to accidents and "stupid" comments, who models for him anything but perfection but who offers him a compassionate heart. (He is never hungry at his mother's table; Janine sees his vulnerabilities, accepts them, and suddenly he is hungry enough to accept her offer of breakfast.) And finally he forms a connection with his father, who is able by the end of the film to name the question that has been dogging him and to face some of his own feelings.

Conrad and Calvin at the film's conclusion are able to express their feelings to one another—to accept that bad things happen in life and that they sometimes happen whether or not we are careful (belying the myth of control). Father and son find a new closeness with each other, thereby in effect rewriting the family rules. Beth chooses instead to resist any change—ostensibly because she wants to hold on to what she's got. Sadly, in trying to hold on to everything to keep herself safe, she loses everything.

In this story of "ordinary people" we can see how the dance of life can be turned into an orderly procession that gives the illusion of beauty and control but which undermines any spontaneity and intimacy, any sense that life, though at times overwhelming, can also be all right. This procession sabotaged any sense of his own individuality that Conrad might have had. The mystery of life flourishes in the delicate balance of being "strange" and connected at the same time. Conrad's strangeness was unacceptable, and his connection was tenuous at best—dependent upon how well he upheld the family system.

There are certain obvious rules that govern this procession, this dance that becomes a march: Don't talk about problems, which means, on the one hand, talk only about problems that do not threaten the order and, on the other, don't have any problems at all—creating the paradoxical illusion that life is controllable and that some problems are just too horrible. Don't talk about or express feelings, especially uncomfortable feelings such as sadness, grief, anger. Don't be selfish; family loyalty comes first, effectively eroding any sense of an individual's mysterious strangeness, any attention to one's own need. Don't rock the boat. (Since life *is* being on a rocky boat, this rule—to avoid creating any turbulence/conflict—is a basic refusal of life.) Have unrealistic expectations for yourself: always be strong or good or perky or perfect. Always be a winner, and then you never have to deal with the pain of defeat or the reality of vulnerability! If anything in life goes wrong, assume someone is to blame. This allows the illusion that life is under control. Avoid direct, honest communication. By talking about school, or the weather, or your performance, we can avoid talking about how we feel.

Families can deny children's feelings and curiosities in a variety of ways, often without realizing they are doing it. A friend who is a pediatrician relates the following scenario:

[A] frequently repeated phenomenon occurs when an older sibling (usually age 3-4) accompanies the new baby to the office for a visit. Often, the older sibling will engage in some conduct which tells me just how angry he/she is that this new . . . interloper has come into his/her home: behaviors like stealing the baby's pacifier, tossing the baby's bottle in the trash can, throwing a bootie at the baby's face or pinching the baby's toe. Inevitably, the mother says, "Now, don't do that David. You know that you love your baby sister." Then I'll say something like: "I'll bet David loves his sister sometimes but other times feels very angry at her for competing with him for your affections." By now David is usually bending back the baby's fingers even as his mother is saying, "Not my David; he loves his baby sister."[8]

A mother turns to her son at dinner as he begins to raise a potentially disruptive topic for discussion and asks him, "Are you sure you want to raise that issue?"—thus giving the confusing message that she is uncomfortable with what he wants to say and making it sound as if it is his idea to be silent. A father never praises his children in front of them for fear that they might "think too much" of themselves, thus giving the impression that he is not proud of them at all and that feeling good about oneself is dangerous.

Not all family systems are as pretty as Beth Jarrett's or as seemingly benign as the above examples. In some families, control is exercised with an iron hand. For instance, in Pat Conroy's story *The Great Santini*, the father, who is both a Marine officer and an alcoholic, runs his family as if it were a military unit: expecting perfection, success, obedience, and (for the boys) no tears—meanwhile expecting the same for himself. He seems to have no insight into his children's feelings as he physically intimidates them, particularly his older son. He ridicules his son's lack of resistance to this intimidating behavior by calling him a girl, telling him that a man would rise to the confrontation and fight. He indoctrinates his son into manhood on his eighteenth birthday by getting him drunk and bullying him into ruthlessly injuring an opponent on the basketball court, thereby cajoling the son to replicate his father's behavior. As a result of his father's continual pressure, the son is confused about who he is and to whom he should listen. He struggles continually with his own feelings until, at the end of the story, he has finally become his father's son.[9]

Sometimes family systems that operate by these life-denying rules are grounded in and mirror larger religious or cultural systems that also practice and reinforce these rules. When my daughter Christina was in second grade, I visited her school and was appalled to see that she was required to go to the bathroom by class schedule: children stood on line to do what the teacher said, when she said it. While our family operated by a different set of rules, I wondered what the effect of this conditioning would be on her and on her friends who did not have modeled at home a system that encouraged children to listen to their own needs. Similarly, Anne Wilson Schaef relates the story of how one of her clients came to see the rules of not feeling, etc., the way they led to a condition of non-living, and the way the church and family worked together to enforce them:

> She told me that she had grown up in a Southern state and had been raised in a fundamentalist Christian church. Her home and her church were the primary formative institutions in her childhood. In both places, whenever she was "alive"—happy, noisy, full of energy, excited, exuberant, sexual—she was labeled a "bad girl." But whenever she was "dead" or nonliving—quiet, sick, depressed, and showing none of the other signs of "life"—she was labeled a "good girl." She learned that to be alive was bad and to be nonliving was good. To be accepted by her world, she had had to be personally powerless and not alive.[10]

The effect of living in any of these systems is in fact to feel powerless and not alive.

In the story of Beth and Conrad Jarrett we ostensibly see two types of responses to living in a system that denies the vicissitudes of life and seeks to control life (eroding its mystery). On the one hand we see Beth, who responded to the system by mastering it—in fact, seeking pretty successfully to fulfill its rules. On the other hand we see Conrad, who does not succeed in the family system. He suffers instead with the sense of not being enough. Unable to learn the choreographed dance, Conrad instead drags his feet. And, overwhelmed by his inability to deal with life's messiness and ambiguity, he attempts to kill himself.

While the two responses seem to be different, they are in many ways the same—for living in such a system has meant to both of them that neither has the skills to meet life on its terms and to enjoy the ride. Both experience life as a battlefield. Their different responses, born of a similar brokenheartedness, mask a terror within: life will get me eventually if I don't—or life is overwhelming me because I can't—keep it under control. The responses mask a refusal of the face of the other: if I truly see his face, I will see that I'm not in control; if I truly see her suffering and limits, then I will have to face the fact that she may not be able to love me in a way that I need. They mask the inability to let another see me: if he sees me he will see my pain and either reject me or be overwhelmed by my feelings— and then I'll see them, too, and be overwhelmed as well. Finally, the responses mask a "stuckness" in an either-perfect-or-a-failure, either-winner-or-loser, either-in-control-or-overwhelmed approach to life, without a range of other possible responses (or the experience of not being perfect and being met with acceptance and humor), and a denial of the mysterious way life can heal (and be "worth it" despite the pain). Raised in a system that did not teach her to embrace the messiness of life which was also a refusal of herself and her own messiness, Beth sought to control it; raised in the same system, Conrad at first succumbed. Ironically, this system is one that promised freedom from life's turbulence. Instead it brings not freedom but slavery to the choreographed dance that becomes a march of death.

In his book *In Over Our Heads*, psychologist Robert Kegan talks about family systems as a religion that teaches family members about life. He has said: "Every family is a naturally and unself-consciously religious place because every family is a place where day after day, year after year, a coherent and often undeviating disposition toward ultimate reality is being expressed." If Kegan is correct, then the type of family system that we see in the lives of Beth and Conrad Jarrett is one that teaches that the "Life Force" is not generous or unforgiving (why else would they need to be so perfect?) and that being alive is dangerous—and only exhilarating when it is under control.[11]

Learning to Dance Again

In my family, the family secret that we were not allowed to talk about was that my mother was in a wheelchair. Her wheelchair was the governing fact of all of our lives: our comings and goings were determined by whether locations were handicapped-accessible, whether we could find a large enough parking place, and the fact that my mother needed more assistance than a physically able woman might have needed. But while this fact was central, our thoughts and feelings about it were taboo. We did not talk about how we felt when children stared at us as we pushed Mother's wheelchair, or when folks would tell us how lucky we were to have such a courageous mother. Nor did we discuss the other losses that came along with her inability to walk. (We took no vacations. She wasn't able to teach us how to swim—although I do remember one night lying stiffly across a kitchen chair and practicing "the crawl." We children often had to watch out for one another.) On the one hand, these were not unreasonable losses or responsibilities. Families do and should pull together and help each other out. But at times they felt unreasonable and overwhelming—and my dilemma as the oldest child was what to do with those feelings. How could I share them when my mother's polio was not her fault, and when even talking about it might make her (or me) feel bad? And whom could I talk to when my dance became a march of resignation— the walk of someone who does what she has to because she feels she has no other choice?

There are, of course, family systems and family secrets other than the types with which I was raised. Alcoholic families seek to "cover up" the alcoholic's behavior, and children of alcoholics learn coping behaviors to keep drinking episodes under control. Families with sexual and physical abuse will lie to obscure the perpetrator's be- havior—calling a black eye the result of walking into a door, or claim- ing that a burn on a face is from too much sun rather than the result of a cup of scalding hot chocolate thrown across the room.

Reneé was a vivacious member of her local youth group. Her father was one of the deacons of the church, a Sunday school teacher, and the first to stand up on Sunday evenings and give testimony to God's activity in his life. Her father also beat her mother and her two brothers and had an incestuous relationship with Reneé from the time she was eight. Reneé never talked about this reality. Her approach to life was to be outside the family unit as much as pos- sible. But when she was sixteen, her father's abuse escalated, and at a church retreat she confided the truth to the youth worker. While this young woman sided with Reneé and sought to give her support (this occurred before the passing of legislation requiring ministers to report instances of abuse such as this), she was constantly thwarted by the family in her attempt to deal with the issue (the mother de- nied the abuse; a rich uncle, whose name was important in the com- munity, offered to send Reneé away, trying to save the family name) and by the church (the pastor denied that the situation was even possible).

I did not have anyone to share my feelings with when I was a child—nor did I even know the questions that my experience raised for me until much later in life, when I had someone to help me and I could begin to heal. Similarly, Conrad Jarrett began to dance again when he was no longer alone, when he found new relationships that allowed him to see the rules under which he had been living, and when he was offered the opportunity to envision, experience, and practice alternate rules by which to live. In the office of Dr. Berger or with Janine, he discovered a new freedom to be and to express himself. He discovered, when he was free to talk about his feelings, that he had been living in a stifling system that had denied him his feelings and was unable to give him the support he needed to dance the dance of mystery with which we began this chapter. He learned that life sometimes hurts, that feelings would not kill him, that he could be clumsy and awkward, that he had talents he was not even aware of when he was trying to be the perfect kid that his parents could be proud of, and that even though life was at times dangerous (he had been in the boat with his brother when his brother had drowned), he had in fact survived. Yes, life could be unpredictable and overwhelming, but he could survive. He also learned that he could love his mother despite her inability to express her feelings toward him, that he had very little power over whether she was able to love him back, and that the fact wouldn't kill him.

As with the other examples of brokenheartedness in this section, healing from the dance of control entails becoming conscious of our own nonliving (to borrow Schaef's phrase), attending to the source of our pain and facing it, making new relationships, and discovering new rules for living, a new range of responses to what life brings. Ironically, it is sometimes the very pain of nonliving we would seek to control that can be the key to this discovery. It was when Conrad could not succeed in his family system, and when he realized that he was dying in it, that he began looking for help. In this case, we might say that to fail was to win. It was in the context of that help that he was able to begin to live again in the faith that, to use Kegan's words, life in all its vulnerabilities and in spite of its danger is also exhilarating.

Sin and the Dance of Control

This exploration into family systems and how they refuse both the individual and the mysterious workings of life raises several more questions for us about the relationship between brokenheartedness and sin.

First, while many Christians may think it is the mark of the saint to be perfect, we can see in the story of Beth Jarrett that the desire to be perfect can reflect the need to be in control and can cover a heart that is broken because life is not safe , a heart that has refused the messiness that is "me." If "control" is anything like the sin of pride, then we must ask where the sin of pride might be rooted.

Second, at the root of controlling behavior lies a despair—a despair born not just from life's vicissitudes, but also from not having had nurtured in oneself an appropriate resiliency to life's pulls and tears. To nurture resiliency in our children is an act of faith that the mystery of life can be trusted, as can our ability to respond to life. To be taught control (a control that means we ourselves must also be under control—with our rough edges and messy parts tucked away) erodes this mystery and our ability to receive it as such.

Third, the dance that becomes a march is meant to be liberating—freeing one from the vicissitudes of life. In actuality it is the lockstep of slavery—of bondage to a way of life that is death.

Fourth, this slavery is inherited—passed on from generation to generation, both by the modeling of controlling behavior and the enforcing of rules of control, and by the failure to nurture the processes that are grounded in the mystery of life and that could in some way sustain it.

Finally, the dance of control raises the question of whether a world that is scary enough to evoke responses of control and despair can in fact be trustworthy at all. Perhaps the response of control is both understandable and—given life's scary and dangerous aspects—the best we can do. And so, to talk of mystery and the overwhelmingness of life is to ask the questions: How do we then live in good faith? And who is the God in whom we trust?

---

[1] Robert Kegan, *In Over Our Heads: The Mental Demands of Modern Life* (Cambridge, Mass.: Harvard University Press, 1994), p. 267.

[2] See Beverly W. Harrison, "The Power of Anger in the Work of Love: Christian Ethics for Women and Other Strangers," in *Making the Connections*, Carol Robb, ed. (Boston: Beacon Press, 1985), pp. 3–21.

[3] To speak of an openhanded approach to life is not to suggest that life cannot from time to time be dangerous, necessitating defending ourselves. Part of the dance of life is in fact to determine when life is dangerous and when it is not. A perfectly appropriate dance step is the dance of what Dana Gold once called "bubbling up"—putting on one's protective shield.

[4] The erosion of wonder, the way we fail to see the beauty and mystery of life, is reflected in Thornton Wilder's *Our Town* (New York: Coward-McCann, 1938). We remember Emily's pain as she sees how much human creatures miss in their daily lives. She says: "Oh, earth, you're too wonderful for anybody to realize you. Do any human beings ever realize life while they live it—every, every minute?" And the stage manager replies: "No. The saints and poets, maybe—they do some" [Act Three].

[5] See Jessica Benjamin's *The Bonds of Love* (New York: Pantheon Books, 1988), for an exploration of the importance of the first bonds of love in a person's ability later in life to establish open, intimate, and respectful relationships.

[6] I first became interested in family systems and rules and the critique of how they function through Robert Subby's book, *Lost in the Shuffle: The Co-Dependent Reality* (Pompano Beach, Fla: Health Communications, 1987). This book about codependence argues that the root of codependence is in dysfunctional families of all types that have in common certain rules that shape people in dysfunctional (and for him addictive) ways. His list of rules forms the basis for my own.

I have chosen to avoid, however, the discussion on codependence. My perception is that the term codependence has grown so large—to cover such a wide variety of behaviors—as to be unmanageable. However, the notion that addictions—compulsive, controlling behaviors—are born of family (or other) systems that refuse children (teaching them to deny their feelings and problems, and leaving them often with the sense that their problems are overwhelming) and are the schools in which people learn alienating behavior (to march rather than to dance) is one I still find compelling. See my "Dysfunctional Families: Schools for Sin?" in *Church and Society*, May/June 1992, Vol. LXXXII, No. 5, pp. 13–24.

[7] The fact that the character of Beth Jarrett was intended by director Robert Redford to be honed down to this stark sort of orderliness is reflected in Mary Tyler Moore's memory that Redford was concerned that her image as "Mary Richards" from her popular television series not be seen as affecting the character of Beth (and by implication make Beth funnier and more likable). See the review of Moore's autobiography *After All* by Diane Rafferty in *The New York Times*, Dec. 3, 1995, sec. 7, p. 14.

[8] From the notes of Dr. Ev Vogeley. Used with her permission.

[9] Pat Conroy, *The Great Santini* (New York: Bantam Books, 1976, 1987).

[10] Anne Wilson Schaef, *When Society Becomes an Addict* (San Francisco: Harper & Row, 1987), p. 16. Schaef also points out that this message to be "nonliving" often is directed particularly at women. In her earlier book *Women's Reality: An Emerging Female System in the White Male Society* (Minneapolis: Winston Press, 1981), Schaef's description of the White Male System is an example of a cultural system that enforces life-denying rules and that erodes the mystery of life (for instance, in its rules of perfection and omnipotence).

[11] Kegan, *In Over Our Heads*, p. 267.

Chapter 7

Sin and the Broken Heart

As [Jesus] walked along, he saw a man blind from birth. His disciples asked him, "Rabbi, who sinned, this man or his parents, that he was born blind?" Jesus answered, "Neither this man nor his parents sinned; he was born blind so that God's works might be revealed in him. We must work the works of him who sent me while it is day; night is coming when no one can work. As long as I am in the world, I am the light of the world." When he had said this, he spat on the ground and made mud with the saliva and spread the mud on the man's eyes, saying to him, "Go, wash in the pool of Siloam" (which means Sent). Then he went and washed and came back able to see. The neighbors and those who had seen him before as a beggar began to ask, "Is this not the man who used to sit and beg?"

—John 9:1–8

In this story of the healing of the man born blind, Jesus effectively severs the question of evil from that of the man's sin: neither the man's sin nor that of his parents, Jesus says, was the cause of the man's blindness. In responding to the disciples' question in this way, Jesus also lets his disciples know that their wrangling over the question of sin—of who is guilty, who to blame—can divert them from the real focus of his work. Don't get sidetracked, he is saying, but watch and see what is God going to do next. This is the gospel.

In a similar fashion, we have seen in both our discussion about sin and our chapters on brokenheartedness that conscientization—coming to consciousness of a new possibility and seeing the old in the light of that new (what we might call God's new possibility)—is crucial to the process of healing, being made new. In the light of God's new possibility, we see our sin, confess, and seek forgiveness;

in the context of a new type of relationship, brokenhearted ways of relating to ourselves and others are revealed, and we are freed to relate to ourselves and others in a new way.

When we focus on God's grace in this way (assuming that we can conflate the experiences of healing of brokenheartedness with God's graceful activity in the world), then the question of whether brokenheartedness is sin or something else seems to be a distraction. Our focus need not be on guilt or blame, but on the new things God is doing right now. In the context of that grace, we can give up our old ways of being in the world and celebrate new life.

But while questions of blame and guilt *are* often more paralyzing than liberating and can actually reflect systems of control that need to blame someone or something whenever something goes "wrong," they also can be liberating. A child who has carried a burden of guilt for his parents' divorce can be greatly relieved to hear that he was not the cause of the rift. A student who feels that there is something the matter with her because she doesn't fit into the academic world of her choice can be liberated (as well as angered) to learn that it is the system which has not yet adjusted to having women in the classroom, that is the source of her distress and not anything she has done (except enroll in the program). A teacher who is pointedly asked by an African-American student why there aren't more texts from an African-American perspective assigned on the syllabus can perhaps respond less defensively when she realizes not only that she has made a mistake but that her mistake reflects her conditioning in a racist society. (This is not an excuse to be racist but an admission that sometimes our behavior is embarrassingly more reflective of unjust systems than we are always aware.)

The question of blame or guilt—or of responsibility, as I will prefer to call it—is especially crucial for those caught in dances of alienation like those we have discussed in this section: those whose activities hurt others and themselves are born out of a broken heart. It is also crucial for churches who call people to confess their sins as if that is the only way to identify human alienation and heal its brokenness. For example:

Cheryl is a single parent of three children. She was raised in a family that abused her. She was denied the "good enough" loving she needed by her mother; her father physically abused her and carried on an incestuous relationship with her. Cheryl suffers from an overwhelming sense of self-loathing, a desire to hurt herself (she burns herself periodically with cigarettes), and an inability to care properly for her own children. She once physically abused her oldest child and fears that this could happen again. Realizing that she needs help, Cheryl joins a support group for parents who are themselves recovering from childhood sexual abuse. This group meets weekly in the basement of a local church. She has been reluctant to attend these meetings because as a child she learned in church that she was full of original sin. This argument was used by her father from time to time to justify his abuse of her as his way of keeping her "sinful self" in line.[1] She has also been taught that sex outside marriage is a sin. Because this category of "sex outside marriage" is the only category she has had to understand her incestuous relationship with her father, she has feared that all the church has to tell her is that she has sinned. She hasn't wanted to come to a meeting and hear again that she is a sinner. She already knows that!

At her first meeting, Cheryl is shocked to hear the leader of the group tell her that although sex outside marriage might be sinful, not all "partners" bear equal culpability for the sin, and that a child in an incestuous relationship is not guilty of sin but the victim of someone else's sin. Hearing that a child's ambivalent feelings about her abusing parent—wanting to be touched and held, but not in "that" way—reflect a normal human desire for affection and affirmation, and that the awful feelings victims often have about themselves (and the blame they assume is theirs) often cover their brokenheartedness at what someone who is supposed to love them and keep them safe has done to them, Cheryl finds a new category to help her understand herself. She has found a way to begin to unpack the layers of shame, anger, and guilt, both appropriate and inappropriate, that are all packed into her life, and a hope that she actually might not deserve all the abuse she has learned to give herself and accept from others.

Jim was a pastor of a large urban church. He also had been an alcoholic for ten years. Both of his parents were alcoholics, and Jim had sworn as a child never to drink. However, with a possible genetic predisposition to alcoholism, combined with being depleted by the years of exposure to his parents' drinking habits, and brokenhearted over the love he never could squeeze out from them no matter how good he tried to be, Jim had turned to alcohol as a way to manage his fears that life was too large for him to handle. He thought he had kept his drinking under control, not letting it interfere with his work. But one Sunday he showed up too sick to lead worship, and one of his deacons pulled him aside and confronted him with the truth: "You have a drinking problem, Jim, and you'd better face it and get some help fast." Almost relieved that the truth was revealed (but also greatly ashamed of himself), Jim called on another pastor in the area for counsel. Telling his story, Jim was overcome with shame and asked his friend: "How can anyone as sinful as I am be called into ministry?" His friend looked thoughtfully at Jim—seeing right through to the brokenheartedness behind the shame—and replied: "Jim, do you know that God is loving you right now? Can you look into God's face and feel God's love?" Jim broke down into sobs at the thought that God might love him but couldn't bring himself in his imagination to even glance in God's direction. That anyone should look at him with love was more than he could stand.

Are the Dances of Alienation Sinful?

Is the language of sin either accurate or helpful in understanding and healing the dances of alienation we have looked at in this section? Does Dan sin when he binds away pieces of himself in order to protect himself from further shaming? Does Paul's mother sin as she sees criticism in the eyes of her children and cannot find it in her heart to love them as she knows she should? Does Beth sin as she struggles to protect herself and her family from the messiness of life?

We have defined sin as a refusal to be who we are (our refusal to accept our humanity with all our possibility and vulnerability), which becomes sedimented into postures of refusal and is acted out in violation of others' lives (as well as our own). We also have said that sin is the refusal of the "something more" that is the ground of the mystery of life and the unfolding of ourselves—a posture that infects the relationships we have and structures with which we come into contact. (It also is a posture learned from structures and relationships that are our context for living.)

At first glance, it might seem that the language of sin is appropriate for understanding the dances of alienation. If sin is the refusal to accept our humanity with all our possibility and vulnerability, then each of the dances reflects such a refusal. The dance of shame is an attempt to correct for the vulnerability of the human condition that has left one so painfully exposed. (I will not let anyone see my enthusiasm ever again!) It reflects an assumption that we can in fact protect ourselves from further shaming, thus denying our vulnerability. The dance of control similarly reflects a desire to deny the messiness of life—whether that messiness is sadness, anger, sexuality, or the hard fact that at times, despite our best efforts, painful things do happen. Both of these dances entail a refusal of our human vulnerability.

The dance of the generations presents a different twist as a dance of alienation. The loyalty to the family myth, the desire to earn the parents' love no matter what the cost, is a different type of refusal. Although it is an attempt to refuse our basic vulnerability (the desire for the parents' love reflects the experience of vulnerability we all suffer without that love, and thus is an attempt to avoid that vulnerability), it is also a refusal of our uniqueness and our possibility, which might strain the family system and risk further refusal. If to be human is to have a unique center of being and certain possibilities that only we can bring to the world, the dance of the generations denies those possibilities, refusing our full humanity.[2]

Second, we can see that each dance of alienation seems like sin, for each also is a sedimented posture of refusal. To speak of such a dance is to speak of a series of learned steps, a choreography, a dance that reflects both a certain construal of the world (the world is dangerous; it will shame me, reject me, or overwhelm me) and a learned response to protect one from that world. This dance is more than a free response to the world; it is one that is learned and invested with terrible significance. It is a practiced posture of refusal.

Third, if sin means postures of refusal that are acted out in violation of others and ourselves, then each dance of alienation we have explored would seem to be sinful. The dance of shame is a violation of oneself as one learns to stifle parts of oneself, to construct oneself in distorted ways, and to deny oneself the very relationality that might possibly heal the wound. It also is often a violation of others as defensive strategies are acted out against those who have shamed us, those who we fear might shame us, or those who are as vulnerable as we were when we were first shamed. The dance of control is also both a violation of our own humanity (denying our own messiness and failing to develop any skills at meeting life's messiness) and a violation of those upon whom we inflict our control. Similarly, the dance of the generations, whether intended or not, is an act of violation where one generation depletes the members of the next generation of the love they need so that they can fill their own needs. Each of these dances constricts its participants and those upon whom it is inflicted and cuts them off from any ability to accept and grow with the mysterious flow of life, the "something more" that is the rhythm of life, the source of all life, the unfolding of their own lives.

Fourth, each of these dances reflects the paradox that dances of alienation are both inherited (something that is passed from one generation to the next, something in which one participates before one is conscious enough to make another choice) and something in which those suffering the alienation are complicit. In each of these dances, the dancer has participated in his own alienation, sometimes through dancing the steps modeled for him, sometimes through adopting his own protective stance, sometimes through dancing whatever steps he needs to remain secure, to keep from being abandoned. His alienation is both an inheritance and a creation of his own. As inherited alienation, these dances would seem to reflect the paradox of the doctrine of original sin: that sin is both something that is inherited and something for which the individual is responsible.

Fifth, each of these dances of alienation reflects a quality of bondage and dividedness that sounds like a description of the bondage and dividedness of sin. As the apostle Paul reflected on sin as a situation in which we are divided against ourselves—with one part knowing what is right, the other resisting those directions—and how this situation is one in which we are stuck, unable in this battle with ourselves to resolve and save ourselves,[3] so each dance reflects both an inner division and a paralysis. As we put away those pieces of ourselves that caused our shame (the part that drew the shame in the first place and which we now fear will not obey the part of us that knows better) and are stuck in our vigilant posture to protect ourselves and cut ourselves off from any source of help, as we abandon ourselves in order to earn a love that can't be earned and that continually eludes our best efforts, and as we deny what is messy in life (including parts of ourselves) and attempt the impossible task of keeping life under control, we are at battle with ourselves and caught in our alienation. This sounds like the bondage of sin.

Sixth, we have seen how the various dances of alienation reflect an idolatrous stance toward the world, effectively turning something that can offer only relative security—or which is not meant to secure but, perhaps, delight—into something we must have or control. Thus the drive for perfection, the desire to find someone who will always love us, the attempt to bracket the messiness of life are all idolatrous postures that deny the vulnerability and possibility of our lives and would therefore seem to be sinful.

Finally, we could argue that the dispute over original intention—that these dances of alienation did not begin with the willful intention of alienation and violation but with the opposite intention of connection—is not an argument against the appropriateness of the name sin for the dances of alienation. Rather, it may accurately reflect the anguish of the human situation where human sin means that we often end up mired in systems of alienation, dancing joyless steps of bondage, when that was never our intent at all. If sin is the human attempt to secure ourselves in the face of the tragic conditions that human creatures are born into—a condition that means conflict and loss, vulnerability, and the desire to be truly and deeply loved in the most fulfilling way—and if the dances of alienation we have described do in fact reflect an attempt by persons, no matter how young and vulnerable, to secure themselves and to gain the love they so deeply need, then the name sin would seem to be appropriate.

Yes, But...

Although these dances of isolation look and sound like sin, in one important way they first of all do not fit the definition of sin.

Unlike the classical tradition that has understood sin as coming from a willfulness born of a desire to be like God (that is then passed on to later generations as a defective will), and unlike the tragic tradition that has understood sin to be the human response of refusal to the precondition of sin that is the tension between our finitude and our freedom, these dances of isolation are born not of a refusal, but of a situation of *being refused*. We are relational, vulnerable beings, and that relationality, we have said, is not insignificant.[4] It is in fact the precondition, the matrix, out of which the dances of alienation are born.[5] If these dances are sin, then they are sin born of a broken heart. Because sin language has often been used to rationalize suffering (suggesting, for instance, that "I must have done something awful to deserve this"), thus hiding the damage and brokenheartedness, this distinction is crucial.[6]

Second, we have acknowledged that the inherited character of these dances sounds like the doctrine of original sin. However, whereas the doctrine of original sin spoke of an inherited defect—a depravity that we inherit just by being born human, the dances of alienation speak not of depravity but of deprivation—and of a deprivation that has a historical location. Despite the fact that inherited dances of alienation feel as if they are synonymous with our being (describe who we are), we have seen that each of the dances is rooted in a time or place and is healed when that root is discovered and the deprivation is mourned and healed. From the perspective of these alienations, if in our brokenheartedness we act in willful ways (and each dance is in its own way a willful dance), then we do so not because we have inherited a defective will, but because we were born vulnerable and into systems that refused us and neglected our brokenheartedness.[7]

Third, while the dances of alienation reflect a dividedness of the person and a bondage to alienation from which we (in the strategies we have adopted, our dances of alienation) cannot extricate ourselves—a bondage that sounds like a traditional understanding of human bondage to sin—this dividedness actually reflects a different battle than the one Paul knew (or, perhaps, a different interpretation of the same one). Paul, we can assume, identified with the part of himself that knew the good and could not do it (that is, for Paul the disobedient self is the problem). His struggle then was to try to get this disobedient part of himself to obey his best knowledge. Although the struggle for Paul is a deadly one, the fact that there is a part of himself that knows the good is a source of comfort. It is what identifies him with God. (He may not be able to *do* the good, but at least he knows what it is!)

From the perspective of these dances of alienation, however, our understanding of the battle of the divided self in the context of brokenheartedness is reversed. These dances reflect a proclivity on our part to protect ourselves from more brokenheartedness by judging ourselves and hiding parts of ourselves away (or abandoning ourselves as we were abandoned). This is done under the assumption that it is those parts of ourselves (and not the systems into which we are born) that are the source of our brokenheartedness. In these cases, the self that judges the other part of the self is not good news for the individual. Rather, the judging self is the self that creates the split in the first place and begins the dance of alienation which, because it seeks to achieve what by definition it cannot achieve— shamelessness, love, perfection and control—is a dance of bondage. Although it perceives the other self to be the problem, it actually is itself the problem (or, more correctly, the symptom of the problem that is its initial refusal).

Whereas in both scenarios the split in the self is a problem that must be healed, in the dances of alienation healing comes not from forgiving the disobedient self (although we must acknowledge where we have violated others and ourselves), but in accepting that part as a messy and vulnerable but crucial part of ourselves. In this case, the battle between the judging self and the messy, shameful self is both real and a cover-up for what is the real problem: the wounded heart. This would seem to be a complete reversal of the apostle Paul's experience and puts the emphasis less on sin and more on the broken heart.

Fourth, while the dances of alienation we have viewed can be named idolatrous, we would do well to remember the source of that idolatry. Traditionally, idolatry has been understood as the failure to trust God, choosing instead to trust oneself or something close at hand. But trust is not given to the human condition. It is something that is learned, particularly as our environment and especially our parents prove themselves to be trustworthy and treat us in a trustful way.[8] The dances of alienation we have viewed may reflect a lack of the ability to trust, but they do so not because those caught in these dances have chosen not to trust, but because their ability to trust was never developed from the potential with which they were born.

Moreover, Ana-Maria Rizzuto, in *The Birth of the Living God*,[9] has shown how this situation of lack of trust is further complicated because not only our ability to trust, but also our understanding of who God is and how God relates to us, is first formed from early parental relationships. Children actually image God as being like their parents. Without other possible ways of imaging God and understanding their relationship to the source of all life, children can continue to understand God as shaped in their parents' image. It would be very understandable for someone raised by distant and angry parents, who were incapable of loving, to image God in that way. We might say that it is understandable that such persons might find themselves unable to trust in such a God at all. Without help in imaging God in a new way, people can be in bondage to the graven images formed in their childhoods.[10]

Finally, we must remember our argument in chapter 3 that behavior becomes sinful only in the light of a new possibility. The dances of alienation we have explored in this section were born out of a need to survive, often when the child had no other options. It is only later when the child/adult is no longer subject to the same danger—and/or a new way of being is possible but the person still clings to the old way of being—that language of sin might be possible.[11] Paradoxically, what first might have been a God-given way of coping becomes instead a pattern of refusal and the grounds of sin. One who responds to that new possibility may then choose to name the earlier alienation as sin. This might even be a tactic that allows those caught in alienation to acknowledge that, because they are complicit in their alienation, they can also then participate in their healing. Some, however, might feel that the language of sin would cover the reality of their refusal and their grief over their brokenheartedness.

And, So...

In her helpful book *Despair: Sickness or Sin?* Mary Louise Bringle comes to the conclusion that despair—a despair that sounds very much like the dances of alienation we have explored in this section— can be thought of as both sickness and sin and that, probably, both ways of addressing the situation of despair are helpful.[12] Perhaps in the way we now know that light is both a wave and a particle, rather than one or the other, the dances of alienation we have explored can be seen both as sin and as the acting out of a broken heart.[13] And those who sin out of a broken heart can be understood as both victims (those who have been refused) and sinners at the same time. This does not diminish responsibility for sinful behavior, but it complexifies our understanding of human sin and allows us to understand how sometimes we are sinners despite our best intentions (our desire to gain another's love) or at least when our intention was not to violate another but simply to secure ourselves against the world's refusal.[14] It also invites us to realize that sometimes when we sing of the sinfulness of the world, we are speaking not only of our human proclivity to sin, but of the brokenheartedness that sin inflicts on others and ourselves.[15]

"I'm depraved on accounta I'm deprived," says a character from Stephen Sondheim and Leonard Bernstein's *West Side Story*. And, indeed, the intent of this section has been to raise the question of how deprivation, dances of alienation, and sin are related. By exploring these three dances of alienation, we have seen how dances of alienation have their roots in deprivation, dysfunction, broken relationships, refusals, and abandonment. We have also seen the deep human need to be loved and to love in return, our human vulnerability to refusal, and how we can in turn refuse ourselves as well as others dancing dances of alienation (and how we fear in the process that we are awful persons, unworthy of any love).

If we are to conclude that the dances of alienation we have explored can be said to be sin, my desire in this section has been to stress that they are sin *and* that they are rooted in a broken heart. Thus, dances of alienation cannot *easily* be named as sin. This pushes us to a greater awareness of the ambiguity of the human condition, of the vulnerability that is central to human experience, of the importance (and fragility) of love in the nurturing of our very souls, and of the relationship between love for ourselves and our ability to love (rather than violate and refuse) others.

To a Christian tradition that has tended to understand Jesus' command to "love God, and love your neighbor as yourself" mostly as a *twofold* command, resting in the assumption that love of self comes easily to human persons,[16] the alienations studied in this section can offer another challenge. We might wonder, after viewing the dances of alienation as we have, if perhaps humans do not easily love themselves after all. Perhaps love of self is something learned when we are loved and when our love of others is received and valued. And perhaps what looks to the world like self-love—a sinful self-preoccupation, a desperate need to secure ourselves—is in actuality a dance of alienation as we seek to hide unacceptable parts of ourselves or to be more than we feel that we are in order to present to others, God, and the world a face we hope will be well pleasing. This insight is not insignificant as we consider redemption from sin and the healing of our broken hearts.

---

[1] See Patricia L. Wismer, "For Women in Pain," in *In the Embrace of God*, Ann O'Hara Graff, ed. (Maryknoll, N.Y.: Orbis Books, 1995), pp.138–160, for an argument that the doctrine of sin can be used to rationalize abuse.

[2] In terms of forms of sin, we might say that the dance of control reflects more the sin of pride, the dance of the generations is more the sin of hiding, and the dance of shame is both a pride to control the situation and a hiding of parts of ourselves.

[3] See Romans 7:14–25.

⁴It has been hard to identify where relationality belongs for the theologians of the tragic. It does not appear to figure prominently in the work of Kierkegaard or Niebuhr. Edward Farley, however, in *Good and Evil*, introduces the dimension of the interhuman as a part of the human situation. While Farley still begins his explanation of sin from the dimension of the subjective, he also reflects on the importance of relationality. When we allow relationality to enter into the discussion, our categories of sin and brokenheartedness get messy, as they do in this chapter, and it is at times hard to discern where one ends and the other begins.

⁵Rita Nakashima Brock understands this well when she says: "I am suggesting that sinfulness is neither a state that comes inevitably with birth nor something that permeates all human existence, but a symptom of the unavoidably relational nature of human existence through which we come to be damaged and damage others. Our attempts to avoid that radically relational nature—a thoroughly contingent existence which embeds us in history and society—emerge from our inability to face our own pain and be healed. If we begin with an understanding that we are intimately connected, constituted by our relationships ontologically, that is, as a basic unavoidable principle of existence, we can understand our brokenness as a consequence of our relational existence. This ontological relational existence, the heart of our being, is our life source, our original grace. But we are, by nature, vulnerable, easily damaged, and that vulnerability is both the sign of our connectedness and the source of the damage that leads us to sin" (*Journeys by Heart*, p. 7). I agree with Brock about the vulnerability of our human situation and the inevitability of damage. Because I am not trying to say that the situations I have called the dances of alienation reveal the source of all sinful behavior (they might, or might not), I do not treat them as synonymous with sin. And because I believe that damage can be repaired by those who inflict it, I would say that the source of our alienation is not damage, but unhealed damage, damage that has then been incorporated into cycles of brokenheartedness. I believe that Brock would agree with me on this point.

⁶Donald E. Gowan in "Salvation as Healing," in *Ex Auditu*, Vol. 5, 1989, pp. 1–19, studies the relationship between sickness, sin, and healing in the biblical tradition.

⁷It is, of course, possible to say that our relationality and vulnerability are the defective humanity we inherit. However, we have argued that relationality and vulnerability are a part of life as we are given it (as it was created). To call them a defect would be to name some aspect of creation sinful, and the tradition has consistently resisted doing that.

⁸Erik Erikson, in *Childhood and Society* (New York: Norton, 1950), places trust as one of the seven stages of human development.

⁹Ana-Maria Rizzuto, *The Birth of the Living God: A Psychoanalytic Study* (Chicago: University of Chicago Press, 1979).

¹⁰See Carroll Saussy, *God Images and Self-Esteem: Empowering Women in a Patriarchal Society* (Louisville: Westminster/John Knox Press, 1991) for a fuller description of how God-images are formed, how abuse affects understanding of God, and the other resources/experiences that inform that process.

¹¹In cases where one's behavior is both understandable as an act of survival *and* hurtful to another (or oneself), we might follow Suchocki's distinction between sin and evil. Sin refers to one's consciousness of one's alienation in the context of a new possibility, and evil refers to the damage that is done. See *The Fall to Violence*, p. 94, where she says: "My claim is that without the ability to transcend our violent tendency, there may be evil, but it is not yet sin."

¹²Bringle concludes: "Is despair, then, a sin or a sickness? Our investigations have implied both answers at various points. Or more precisely, our investiga-

tions have led us to the conclusion that despair is neither sin nor sickness *per se*, but rather a *symptom* of both." Mary Louise Bringle, *Despair, Sickness or Sin* (Nashville: Abingdon, 1990), p. 173.

[13] Perhaps the classic example of someone mired in sin whose sin is rooted in a broken heart is Scrooge from Dickens' classic *A Christmas Carol*, mentioned earlier. Through Scrooge's Christmas Eve journey through Christmases past, present, and future, he comes to the triple awareness of just how hard his heart has become, the effects of that hard-heartedness on others (that is, he comes to see his sin), and the brokenhearted childhood at its root.

[14] The notion that we need more than one category to speak about sin from the perspective of victims of sin is not new to me. Mary Potter Engel, in her article "Evil, Sin, and Violation of the Vulnerable" (found in *Lift Every Voice*), argues for two foci in looking at situations of violation: evil (the violation done to one) and sin (the violation we act out upon others and ourselves). Most of us, she notes, are some mixture of the two. In a similar vein, Wendy Farley, in her book *Tragic Vision and Divine Compassion* (Louisville: Westminster/John Knox Press, 1990), introduces the category of "radical suffering" (suffering that is not earned by sin and which violates the soul of the sufferer) along with the category of sin. Andrew Sung Park, in *The Wounded Heart of God*, introduces the Korean *minjung* concept of *han* (and not sin) as a way of describing the alienation of victims.

[15] I find this particularly in the African-American tradition, where spirituals often use the word "sin" to mean both "my sins" and the sin that is inflicted upon "me."

[16] See, for instance, Calvin's *Institutes of the Christian Religion*, trans. by Ford Lewis Battles, ed. by John T. McNeill (Philadelphia: Westminster Press, 1960), III, vii, 5, where he says: "If this [to renounce ourselves] is the one thing required—that we seek not what is our own—still we shall do no little violence to nature, which so inclines us to love of ourselves alone that it does not easily allow us to neglect ourselves and our possessions in order to look after another's good, nay, to yield willingly what is ours by right and resign it to another." I believe that the self-preoccupation Calvin is focusing on in this section on self-denial is the desire to secure oneself (perhaps born of a broken heart) that we have been discussing in this section. We must, then, make a distinction between self-preoccupation and self-love. The problem that Calvin sees is not self-love but a need to secure oneself that is so desperate that it becomes the central (if not only) focus of one's living. His intent is to break open this self-preoccupation by calling people to self-denial and care of others. But, if self-preoccupation is born of a broken heart, then one corrects this self-preoccupation not by self-denial, but by healing which, because it entails the restoration of the human bridge, entails more open and caring commerce between oneself and others.

Part III

I believe that people are attracted to the gospel, not simply repelled by their sins. I have a hunch that the early Christians made converts not by terrifying people with the prospect of judgment, but by vividly depicting a new order of reality which was already bursting upon the world through Jesus. The passion that drove Jesus' disciples to evangelistic zeal was fueled not by the desire to fill heaven with sinless saints but by relief at being liberated from the delusional game played by the powers that be, and by the determination to set others free.

Walter Wink[1]

SALVATION:

Healing Our Broken Hearts

Chapter 8

Healing for Our Broken Hearts

Sin and sickness do come together in Jesus' work, then; not because one is necessarily the cause of the other, but because he came to save us from both. There is more than one kind of healing, and each kind is called salvation: forgiveness of sins, psychological healing, and the healing of physical illness. Each involves a different kind of alienation, but each also has something in common with the others. …What they have in common is the likelihood that the person in need of healing will be alienated from normal community life, sometimes as a result of their own choices, sometimes in spite of their most fervent wishes. The salvation Jesus brought to all who responded to him, as he healed them physically, psychologically and spiritually, was the ability to live a rich and full life, as the Old Testament prophets had hoped.

—Donald E. Gowan
"Salvation as Healing"[2]

The Christian religion has always been about salvation. Sometimes, as Donald Gowan suggests above, that salvation has been healing of body and spirit. Sometimes it has been a new consciousness that entails changed behavior. Sometimes it has meant the forgiveness of sins. Always it has meant the restoration of human beings into full community with themselves, others, and God.

The prophet Nathan tells King David a simple story about a rich man who steals a lamb from his poor neighbor rather than kill one of his own and reveals to David the treachery of his own behavior (2 Samuel 12:1–15a). Jesus tells parables so that people can see in a new way; he eats with prostitutes, tax collectors, and sinners and restores them into community. He heals, and no longer are people isolated from their communities. He dies on the cross, and yet he lives—and people's lives are turned around.

Despite understandings of salvation and reconciliation that have focused on the work of salvation as fulfilling God's system of righteousness or on satisfying God's honor (where the focus is on God), our understanding has also been that salvation is about a change in us. In the light of the gospel narrative, we see ourselves in a new light. In the shadow of the cross, we cry out for forgiveness for the ways we have crucified one another. Seeing on the cross a love that will not abandon us in our sufferings, we dare to hope that crucifixion is not the last word and find courage to work for God's justice on this earth.[3]

At a Lenten dinner, my daughter Christina and I act out an all-too-common occurrence between us in the hope of revealing to the community the ways in which we crucify each other, thereby hoping to evoke both new consciousness and changed behavior in ourselves and others. We pantomime a fight we have had over cleaning up the kitchen. In order to visualize the effect our fighting has had on each of us, we each wear a bib of red construction paper stapled to a ribbon around our necks. As we furiously "tear into" each other in our fight, we also rip off pieces of each other's red paper bib and throw them on the ground. Finally, when the shredded paper catches our attention, we look sadly at each other—realizing in the torn shreds the damage we have done to one another. Finding some tape then, we carefully attach pieces of paper back onto what remains of the bibs around our necks. All the time in our motions we indicate to each other our sorrow and seek forgiveness, each in the other's face. Finally, when we have repaired each other in a good enough fashion, we hug and walk off the stage arm-in-arm, stopping momentarily to remove our shredded but restored paper bibs and to hang them on a cross in the middle of the stage. Seeing the treachery of our ways, we repent and are reconciled. To this day, whenever I begin to lose my temper, I visualize those torn paper bibs hanging on the cross.

Our little pantomime that day was designed to evoke an awareness and a change in people's lives and to make the cross more accessible to the people in our congregation. Maybe, we thought, if they could visualize how their own behavior violates others (if they could see their own sin), then they could look on the cross with new eyes: seeing both their sin and the love of God that would redeem them from their sin. Taking the cross for a moment out of the past and putting it in the midst of our Lenten devotional, we hoped both to make God's grace palpable in their everyday lives and to offer the opportunity for new ways of living.

But our story of the cross was not only the story of sin; it was also the story of brokenheartedness. For those shredded bibs were a visual image of both our sinful behavior toward each other and of the damage we had done to each other. And in our attempt to tape our bibs back together again, we acted out an awareness of that damage, the pain of being damaged, and the importance of healing our broken hearts.

In the previous chapter, I argued that the dances of alienation we have studied can be thought of as both sin and brokenheartedness, and that what looks at times like sin may actually be rooted in a prior experience of being refused. Healing from brokenheartedness may then entail two modes of healing: from sin, and from the damage that has caused the broken heart.

Disease and Illness: Getting to the Root

How are sin and brokenheartedness and their respective healings in the case of these dances of alienation related to one another? Arthur Kleinman's distinction between "disease" and "illness" can be a useful tool in understanding this relationship and in helping us see how important it is for churches to offer not only forgiveness for sin, but also healing from the violence of refusals.

Kleinman, a medical doctor, uses the words *disease* and *illness* in different and distinctive ways. *Disease* he uses to describe "the process of pathology in the body." *Illness* he describes as "that complex web of conscious and unconscious meanings which the patient, his family, the physicians, and the whole culture weave around the experience of disease in the form of stories or narratives."[4] That is, someone who is sick not only suffers from a disease, but also has constructed a meaning around that suffering to which the physician also needs to attend. The healing process needs to take into account both categories of disease and illness in order to be genuinely effective.

For instance, when my first child was six weeks old, she had a temperature of 102 degrees. I was immediately afraid upon taking her temperature that she was going to die and that I (without a car or a friend nearby) was helpless to do anything about it. Of course, I was not totally helpless. Even though I did not have access to a car at that moment, I did have access to the telephone—so I phoned our pediatrician to ask for help. I was told to bring my daughter into the doctor's office as soon as I could. This only mildly relieved my anxiety, since I was unable at the time to reach my husband to bring the car home. Meanwhile, however, the doctor's nurse, realizing that I was a new mother, telephoned me to see how I was doing and to inform me that I could give the baby some aspirin to bring her temperature down while I was waiting for the car to come.[5] I was actually afraid that if her temperature did drop, when I took her to the pediatrician's office, the doctor wouldn't believe that she was sick. My sense of insecurity about myself as a mother was understandably kicked up by this event and was already structured into its meaning. Predictably, by the time we finally arrived at the doctor's office two hours later, my anxiety had gotten the better of me. The doctor took one look at the baby (whose temperature had dropped by that time), announced that she had contracted her first cold, and gave her a shot to send antibiotics through her system. Then he looked at me and asked how I was.

In truth, I was shattered. My baby might have had only a little cold, but in the ensuing hours between the onset of her temperature and finally hearing the diagnosis, I had fabricated several tragic dramas that had convinced me her life was indeed threatened. The doctor talked with me for a while about babies and how they sometimes get high temperatures, and that sometimes they *are* serious, and sometimes they are not. He discussed with me several possible strategies for dealing with the inevitable colds and infections that she would get in the next few years. I left the doctor's office that day feeling more confident as a parent and better able to cope with the cold with which my daughter was suffering. The doctor could have dealt just with the disease, writing a prescription and sending us on our way. Instead, he dealt as well with the "illness"—the meanings I had configured around that disease. We all were the better for this.

Kleinman's categories have been helpful to medical professionals as they seek to more fully care for their patients and as they resist the growing movement in managed care systems to pressure physicians to heal the disease without allowing enough time also to attend to the illness that has been constructed around the disease. Kleinman's categories also can be helpful to us as we explore the relationships between sin and brokenheartedness and insist that healing must be not only for sin but also for broken hearts.

In appropriating Kleinman's categories for theological purposes, however, we will in effect reverse the way in which his work has been used by medical professionals. Whereas physicians may be concerned that they are pressured to deal with the disease at the expense of the illness, we might say that a theology that focuses on sin without attending to brokenheartedness deals more with the illness (the narratives that construct meaning around the disease) than with healing the disease. (Here, of course, Kleinman's categories reach the limit of their usefulness, for all human experiences are constructed. So the distinction between disease as the pathology and illness as the constructed meaning falters at this point.)

The dances of alienation we have explored in Section II all begin in an original refusal. This refusal, we have said, wounds the one who is refused. This wound, I am suggesting, roughly correlates with Kleinman's category of disease. It is the wound that needs to be healed. However, around each wound, we have seen, a narrative dance begins to develop. Those who are shamed determine that some part of themselves must be put away to avoid any more shaming; the children caught in the dance of the generations, seeing refusal in their parents' eyes, determine that they must be different than who they are in order to win their parents' love; the dance of control refuses the mystery of life and of the unfolding of the individual, and is evidenced in a dance that choreographs meaning justifying that refusal. These various dances of alienation (which construct not only protection from more refusal, but meaning for the event—a meaning that is often inaccurate) I am suggesting are the corresponding illness.

However, these dances of alienation we have seen also distort what actually happened in the initial wounding experience—reconstructing the disease, as, for instance, those who are shamed blame themselves for their shame rather than seeing that they might not have deserved the wound they received. The wounded ones then come to believe that there is something the matter with them to deserve this treatment (for instance, that they really must be wretched!). These dances serve to camouflage the initial refusal and the pain it created and in time come to be understood as an accurate reflection of who one is and what life is about.

Because these dances are dances of refusal, continuing the initial unhealed refusal into postures of refusal, we have said that they could be named sin. What the "illness" tells the brokenhearted is that the "disease" behind their wounds is their own wretchedness (sinfulness—perhaps original sinfulness). Thus both the perceived disease (which is not the real disease—the wounding/refusal—but a constructed rationalization of that wounding) and the illness (the dances of alienation) are named as sin.

What I am suggesting is that the disease of the brokenhearted is an original and unhealed refusal and that the language of sin is the narrative that has developed—the illness—to make meaning of that refusal. From this perspective, the language of original wretchedness (which in a classical theological paradigm for original sin names the diseased condition that is passed on to each generation—our depravity)[6] is not the disease, but a constructed meaning to explain the disease (thus, also an illness). Because the disease is excised from sight (it is too painful to remember), it is neither acknowledged nor attended to. But, if Kleinman is correct that effective healing entails dealing both with illness and with disease, then theology, when dealing with these dances of alienation, must cut beneath the levels of rationalization and defense that are the dances of alienation and refuse the subterfuge that they are the disease itself.[7]

Dances of alienation are both refusing and lonely dances. Even when they are danced in tandem with one who is in control, or with the one from whom we may hope to get the love and affirmation we need, they are still very lonely, for those parts we have hidden away cannot be brought to the light (and when they are, the result might be further rejection). When the whole world appears whole and healthy and only "I" appear weak (to "myself" and as "I" see "myself" reflected in other's eyes) and inadequate, "I" can feel even more alone and unworthy—even in a crowd or at a crowded Sunday morning worship service! Healing, then, needs to address this sense of isolation, which is part of both the disease and the illness, and return the wounded ones to full community and to a sense that even when they feel unworthy or actually are "in over their heads" their experience is not an uncommon one for human beings—that they are not different from the human community because of this experience.[8]

Healing the Disease and the Illness

We have seen at the end of each chapter on our dances of alienation, that healing from brokenheartedness entails seeing our alienation, discovering our woundedness, returning our understanding of that woundedness to its historical location (in an event and/or a system), grieving the loss that that refusal meant for us, risking new relationships that might restore the interpersonal bridge, and learning to see and envision new responses to our alienation.[9] In the case of the dance of the generations, the suffering we endure in halting the cycle of alienation can be seen as a price that is paid for the "sins" of that system. This process of uncovering, seeing, feeling, and restoring effectively untangles the disease (the broken heart) from the illness (the narrative dances of alienation that we have developed to make sense of that disease and avoid being wounded again). It then allows the disease to be healed, while the illness is also deconstructed (perhaps appreciated both for its distortion of the originating event and as the survival tactic it was) and a new narrative dance is developed, one that might mediate health and wholeness rather than perpetuating alienation.

But how are we suddenly able to see our alienation when it has been so much a part of us as to seem synonymous with who we are? How can we begin to identify faulty narratives (our illnesses) and generate some new ones?

My experience is that there is a certain mystery to this process. This serendipitously makes sense. If the loss of mystery is a part of the dance of alienation, then why wouldn't its return be the beginning of healing? Those of us who have learned dances of alienation, learn in our dances to see what we expect to see in the world. Trained in rejection, we will be wary of finding it again (and usually will). Taught to reach for perfection, we can find that graded scale wherever we go. Schooled in shame, we will protect ourselves from it in any way we can, even when it is not necessary to do so. We continue the war against being refused, when in actuality the war is long over and the damage already inflicted.

And yet, there are times, some more intentionally structured for healing than others, when for a moment we can begin to see through our faulty constructions and get a glimmer that something else is possible in the world for us. There are times when we are met with acceptance rather than refusal; when we experience an unconditional love that breaks the mold of our expectations; when someone sees behind the masks we put on to face the world's weather and sees our hidden face—and is not repulsed by it. To be human is to be relational, and these mysterious moments begin to restore the relational bridges that were damaged. This process of experiencing something new reflects both the reality that the message coming to us is not the one we have learned to expect, and a surprising ability on our part to be able to see that something new is coming our way. Sometimes this mysterious transformation is mediated to us through relationships that restore a trust in others and an ability to love and accept ourselves that we have not been able to develop before.

Julie and I went to college together. We weren't exactly close; we just did a lot of things together. She was a hard worker, often pushing herself to the point of exhaustion, and rather timid in envisioning for herself what her life might be. We drifted apart after graduation but reunited at our twenty-fifth class reunion. Julie seemed to be less driven than I had remembered her to be—more able to laugh. Thinking that perhaps these changes were simply the vestiges of middle age, I asked her over dinner one night about her life.

Julie told me that when she had graduated from college, she had been scared and depressed. She had taken a job teaching high school. Some days she had enjoyed the challenge; other days she had been overwhelmed by it. She also had struggled with a sense of meaninglessness and a nagging fear that she would never not be afraid.

Soon after college, she met and married Clark. They put together a traditional family package, and Julie threw herself into making everything perfect. She sewed, baked everything from "scratch," volunteered with the church youth group—everything she could think of to make her life full of meaning. But one day Clark left her, and her world fell apart. It was as if her worst fears about herself were confirmed. Those were hard times, but somehow in the ensuing years, Julie learned new tactics to cope with life. She joined a twelve-step group to discuss her compulsion with food and her low self-esteem. She learned on the bad days to take them one day at a time. When she was overwhelmed with fears, she discovered that time by herself in her garden was restorative.

A few years after her divorce, Julie met Rick. Since she had had one failed marriage, Julie was particularly wary of what married life might mean for her. What she discovered only partially took her by surprise. No sooner were Julie and Rick married than she began to be plagued by all her old fears and self-loathing. She felt sure that he must be rejecting her when he was simply reading the newspaper; if she complained about something and he seemed a little hurt, she was confirmed in her fear that she was an awful person.

One night Julie awakened from a bad dream. She turned to Rick for comfort, but he was in a deep sleep and slow to arouse. His lack of response set off a rage in Julie that she hadn't even known she had. She began to yell at him and swing at him, almost as if she wanted to make him hurt as badly as she was hurting from his supposed rejection. Julie was both lost in this rage (out of control) and aware of being full of rage at the same time. She wanted Rick's comfort, but also was afraid of what his response to her rage might be. She told me later that her "training" had led her to expect that Rick might have responded to her rage in one of three ways. He might have sneered at her, calling her crazy, and leave her—confirming in her a sense that she was unacceptable. He could have cowered at her anger like a victim of battery—which would have reinforced her sense that she was truly monstrous. Or he could have hit her back—which would have fulfilled her own sense that being beaten was what she deserved. Instead, Julie told me, Rick reached out for her and firmly held her tight and then gently whispered in her ear, "I love you, Julie. I know you feel frightened, I know you are hurting, but I'm here with you. I'm not going to let you go." Somehow, Rick's words gave Julie just the assurance she needed; she slowly calmed down, amazed at the information that was new to her: that she was frightened (she hadn't realized that) and that her rage had been an expression of that fright. Nor had she ever felt before how deeply hurt she was.

The memory of that night of rage and comfort remained with Julie for many months. She was embarrassed by her anger and by her desire to make someone hurt (and hoped that it would never happen again); but she was also comforted by Rick's response. He had seen her anger for what it was and had helped her to understand herself more clearly—seeing clear through to the wound that she had hidden most of her life. Rick's response was something totally unexpected (and thus mysterious), and it broke the hold of the narrative dance that had covered her woundedness and fright and taught her that she deserved rejection, or that she was indeed a monster. Her rage still erupted from time to time, as did her fright, but she also began to understand them and to practice new ways of dealing with her fears. Rick's response to her that night, because it saw through to her fear and pain and because it was such a departure from what she had learned to expect (and Julie's new response in that she was able to see and accept his acceptance), helped her to see the alienation she had been living in and to feel the deep woundedness at the core of her being. She was not healed of either her disease or her illness that night, but she was able to see them, and that was the beginning of her healing.

Kevin was schooled in shame from the time he was a small child. In his adult life, this shame was reflected in the way he felt responsible for anything that went wrong in life, no matter how benign. When something didn't go as he expected, when he forgot to anticipate a possible response or failed to factor a late bill into the family budget, he would immediately feel that he had been inadequate and believe that others could "see right through" him; he felt totally unworthy of any consolation. When in midlife his wife of twenty-seven years announced that she didn't love him anymore and asked him to move out, Kevin's sense of shamefulness hit a new low. He coped with this by avoiding any human contact that was not absolutely necessary.

However, over the previous years Kevin had also begun to participate in a support group of people with whom he had worked from time to time. This group had been intentional from the time of its formation that it would try to operate by different rules than those most of the members had known throughout their lives (such as the rules of control we discussed in chapter six). This meant that feelings were to be expressed and accepted by the group, that they were not to measure one another by any "counsel of perfection," and that they would remind each other from time to time that life can bring suffering and disappointments for which no one is to blame, and that they were always more than what the awful feelings they might have about themselves at such times would suggest they were.

Several weeks after he and his wife had separated, Kevin attended his group's annual winter retreat. He was wary of participating in discussions (he felt too newly vulnerable), but he hoped that just being around some folks he cared for and who seemed to care for him would erode the awful feelings he had inside. Instead, Kevin was unable to keep his shame and sorrow inside but actually blurted out the truth to his friends in a discussion circle one night. His deepest fear at that moment was that his friends would see his shame, realize that he had been fooling them all along (hiding the awful truth of his shame), and reject him (or treat him as an object of pity—which would be another form of rejection). Instead, what he saw on their faces was compassion and respect; they treated him with dignity—as if his shame did not define his being but only reflected the awful loss that he was suffering (and the meaning he had constructed for himself around it). His pain and shame did not immediately go away, but he came away from that retreat knowing that people had looked upon his shame and loved him in it, remembering that he was more than his shame, even when that was not the way he felt, and hoping that in time he would heal from his deepest wounds and be able to love as he had been loved.

Sometimes we can experience healing in almost mystical moments when something new grabs our souls. Walking in the woods on a snowy evening, we can feel in the tranquillity of the place and time a gentleness that can soothe our troubled hearts; standing on the rim of the Grand Canyon, we can feel connected to something far larger and older than we are, and know a certain comfort. Sometimes even our own creative imaginations (open perhaps to a new possibility from the mysterious source of our lives) can generate a moment of consolation.

Kay had always thought of herself as a well-organized, gracious person. She lived an orderly life, punctually met all her deadlines, neatly balanced career and family, and faithfully responded to others when they called out for her help. And then, in the course of six months, her life support system evaporated. Her youngest child, the last one to leave home, had accepted a job across the country and now, like his siblings, was well ensconced in his own life; her husband had been tragically killed in a hiking accident; and her job, which she had counted on to make some meaning out of her life, was being phased out. Kay began to hate coming home at night to the silence of her newly emptied home.

Sometimes at night Kay would begin to feel a fear that she had not known in a long time—the fear of dissolving, the fear that no one loved her and that she didn't exist anymore. Her losses, which were in themselves a major blow to her, apparently also touched off memories of a more ancient loss and the fears and meanings she had constructed around that loss. When these fears overtook her, she would roll on the floor in pain, sobbing and moaning until the fear abated. One night the pain of her fear felt larger than ever before, and she felt that she was going to die. But then she had a vision. She saw in her imagination a river, a raging river—and in the midst of the river was a dock. And then she realized that she was in the river, holding on to the dock to save her from the raging water. But a voice seemed to say to her, "Kay, let go of the dock." Kay was too terrified to let go. But the voice said to her again, "Kay, let go of the dock." Again Kay refused to let go, yelling out to the voice that if she let go, she would surely drown. And then she heard the voice reply to her, "Kay, you're already drowning." Immediately Kay realized that she had released her hold on the dock and that instead of drowning she was floating down the river—safely buoyed by an ugly brown air mattress. Relaxing on her journey, she was suddenly aware of the beauty of the day—the clear blue sky, the warm and golden sun, the breeze that gently fluttered the aspen leaves. A sense of well-being overcame her and she knew that she was all right.

As Kay looked back on that vision, she could use only the word "love" to describe what had happened to her. Afraid for her life, fearful that life was once again rejecting her as it had done long ago, she released herself into its turbulence and was met by a love that supported her and made her feel safe. She couldn't control what had happened to her life, she realized. But the vision mediated to her a sense that she was neither disintegrating nor invisible. Instead there was something that recognized her, cared for her, and would not let her go.

Julie, Kevin, and Kay all suffered both from a disease and an illness. Their healings came in healing the more ancient disease, deconstructing their meanings (constructed in fear and brokenheartedness), and being restored to community in some form. Each of them experienced through this healing new life—salvation.

Christological Concerns
Just to think of the cross
    moves me now
The nails in his hand,
    his bleeding brow
Just to think of the cross
    moves me now
It should have been me —
    it should have been me,
Instead I am free —
    I am free.
        –Ralph Carmichael
        "A Natural High"[10]

To speak of healing and salvation is to move, theologically speaking, from the doctrine of sin to christology—the doctrine of the person and work of Jesus Christ. This is not the place (at the end of a book on sin) to develop a christology from the context of the brokenhearted. However, we can raise several christological concerns as we consider how we might understand the work of Jesus for those caught in dances of alienation born of the experience of being refused.[11]

First, the cross of Jesus has stood in history as the price of human sin—the cost of our reconciliation—and as a call to confession and forgiveness. It has also been an image that has evoked in believers a change of heart. The poet above is moved by the cross to see the results of his sin, to confess his sinfulness ("it should have been me"), and to claim a new freedom (the power of sin is broken, the cycle has been refused). The blood of the innocent Jesus evokes in the believer the awareness that this never should have happened and that in this new awareness (of his sin, of Jesus' undeserved death, and paradoxically of Jesus' love that would die to end human bondage to sin) he cannot be the same.

Mrs. Davies was my twelfth-grade English teacher. She was greatly admired in our community. To me she was a careful, thoughtful person who, despite her advanced age, was always open to new ideas and experiences. When the rock opera *Jesus Christ Superstar* opened, Mrs. Davies was one of the first to attend. Afterward she told me that it was a marvelous experience but that at the end of the play, as people stood to applaud, she had the sudden feeling that her clapping hands were pounding the nails deeper into Jesus' hands. This both distressed and intrigued her—the thought that she could participate in crucifying Jesus.

To my adolescent mind, Mrs. Davies could never do anything wrong—let alone participate in anything as gruesome as a crucifixion. But as I have reconsidered her response over the years, I have come to suspect that I heard in her comment a new self-awareness of her complicity in structures of evil and even a willingness to name all the ways in which that complicity in fact implicated her in the various evils around her. Moved by the crucifixion scene to see her own participation in history's crucifixions and feeling her participation palpably in her clapping hands, Mrs. Davies, I believe, could not be the same.[12]

The cross *has* been a symbol that has confronted sin and mediated forgiveness and new life. But how can the cross affect those whose disease is a broken heart? Who having been refused, practice dances of alienation that continue the refusal? Who need primarily not forgiveness but the courage to face their woundedness, to see the damage they have wreaked on others and themselves, to understand and deconstruct the meanings they have structured around that damage, to risk new relationships, and to resist forces and systems that continue such refusals?

Second, the cross does not function in the same way for those whose primary disease is a broken heart. Rather, the cross has sometimes served as a tool of further refusal for those who have already been refused. For instance, Delores Williams, in *Sisters in the Wilderness*, names how the cross has not been good news for African-American women in their surrogacy roles—encouraging not freedom and self-affirmation but self-denial and uncritical participation in systems of refusal that drain them of their human dignity.[13] Feminist theologians have argued that crosses of self-sacrifice are not liberating to women whose full humanity has been refused in a patriarchal system and whose primary sin is hiding, flight, or loss of self in the trivialities of life; instead, they argue, it encourages their self-denying (self-refusing) behavior.[14] Rita Nakashima Brock has warned that images of a Father God who demands the death of a son on a cross do not liberate or heal victims of abuse but reinforce their experience of refusal and their fears that the world is one that demands the sacrifice of its children and vindicates the behaviors of their perpetrators.[15] Brock also argues that images of innocent victims reinforce the notion that "victims ought to be innocent, and virtuous or else pain and suffering are deserved"—thereby denying the ambiguity of life, wherein none of us can ever be innocent, and encouraging victims to seek innocence (to be good) rather than to struggle for an end to their suffering (their refusal).[16]

Carol was a student in a "women's experience" course I taught several years ago. The class had been discussing the cross and its model of self-sacrificial love and how it had functioned destructively in many women's lives. After class that day, Carol began to think about a long-standing relationship she was in and how painfully self-denying she had come to be in it. She realized that it would be self-destructive for her to remain in this relationship and thus decided to end it.

At our next class gathering, Carol told us this story. On her way to speak to her boyfriend and to end their relationship, she had a vision of Jesus on the cross. She had always felt close to Jesus—and Jesus on the cross had been an important symbol for her of God's love for her. This Jesus, though, was looking down at her with great anger and said tersely to her, "I've suffered, Carol; why can't you?" This vision was very upsetting, so Carol pulled her car over to the side of the road to settle herself. Then, having decided that the man on the cross could not have been Jesus (for Jesus would not want her to continue to suffer—Jesus was one who healed people and liberated them from their suffering), she continued on her way and broke off the relationship as she had planned.

Carol's vignette reflected a shift in her thinking about Jesus. Jesus her Savior, she said, became larger to her than a cross. (Or, to put it another way, she began to look at more than the cross in seeking a relationship with Jesus.) So she decided to put the cross aside for a while and to begin to look more critically at his *life and ministry,* to see what Jesus might have to say to her as she ventured to be more assertive and self-affirming (as well as other-affirming) in her life.

Carol's shift in thinking regarding Jesus reflects a second christological concern for us. Just as Carol knew intuitively that to speak of Jesus in the context of her alienation she had to look at the life and ministry of Jesus as well as his death on the cross, so a theology that would focus on brokenheartedness as well as on sin must look at Jesus' entire life as well as the meaning of the cross. We must see Jesus not only as one who took upon himself the sins of the world, but also as one whose ministry was to "bind up the brokenhearted"[17] as well. As one who not only forgave sinners, but also, for example, healed lepers from a disease that alienated them from their community.

We read in the Gospel of John (4:1–42) the story of Jesus' meeting with a Samaritan woman at her local well. We can assume that since the Samaritan woman came to the well alone and in the middle of the day (instead of coming with the other women at cooler times), that she was alienated from her community. The story tells us that she had had "many husbands" and that she was currently living with a man who was not her husband. This, we presume, was the source of her shame and what separated her from the other women of her village. We are not told why the woman had so many husbands—perhaps she had been widowed many times; perhaps she was a woman who "loved too much,"[18] who sought an acceptance in the arms of her lovers that would take away an emptiness in her soul. What we do know is that she came to the well alone, met Jesus there, and was not rejected by him. We also know that he knew her story (he knew her shame), that he wanted her to change her behavior, but that he did not treat her as a shameful creature. Rather, he offered her living water. And she, knowing that her story did not merit her rejection and experiencing in Jesus an inclusion in God's kingdom, returns to her village no longer ashamed (he told me everything I ever did, she openly tells the villagers) and preaching good news. (The villagers, of course, are not willing to take her word as the truth and seek out Jesus for themselves. So she is shamed again.)

Third, to look at Jesus through the eyes of the brokenhearted is also to see a rather ambiguous person—one who at times binds up the brokenhearted, while at other times seeming rather aloof to others' feelings. He includes the woman who would wash his feet with her tears while others would refuse her, but he rejects his own mother ("Who is my mother and my brothers?" he asks); he heeds the plea of the Syro-Phoenician woman to heal her daughter, but only after he has first rejected her and compared her to a house-dog; he calls Zacchaeus out of a tree, but he (for no apparent reason) curses a fig tree and it withers.[19] On the one hand, he is called the son of God, with angels announcing his royal birth; on the other, his mother's pregnancy is a shameful one (he was no son of Joseph!). He is visited by wise men but has no extended family to celebrate his birth.[20] He is welcomed into Jerusalem as a king and rejected, beaten, degraded, and shamefully crucified between two thieves.

Fourth, we must reexamine the cross—Jesus' cross of shame—to see if it can speak to the brokenhearted. To see if despite the problems acknowledged before, it can be a healing image for victims of refusal. If Jesus on the cross models dangerous self-sacrificial behavior, might he not also represent God's solidarity with the oppressed and the good news that those who suffer from shame and rejection do not do so alone? If the doctrine of the incarnation tells us that God is not apart from creation but enters the mud and shares it with us, then couldn't the crucifixion be understood to show that God would go as far as the shameful cross to express God's love for the world? If to be shamed is to know awful isolation, to share that shame with God might be to know reconciliation.[21]

Fifth, I would acknowledge here that the cross alone as a symbol of God's solidarity with the refused may not be a strong enough image to heal people of their brokenheartedness. The cross must be not only God's solidarity with the brokenhearted, but a symbol of God's brokenheartedness at a world that crucifies people and God's judgment upon human systems that refuse and crucify—and the resurrection must image God's promise that refusals should not be the last word.[22]

Ann was a second-year seminarian when she began to have memories of childhood sexual abuse. These memories were more than vivid memories; they were also the replay of the betrayal she had known and a reexperiencing of an agony that she described as feeling "abandoned and discarded upon the garbage heap of life." In the midst of this painful time, Ann was asked to help lead a special "celebration of life" in her local church. As she prepared to go to church the night of the celebration, she was involuntarily gripped again by her agony. When she had felt like this in the past, she had usually isolated herself until the pain had passed. This gave her a safe place to grieve and protected her from revealing her agony and shame to others who might reject her. As she considered whether to go to the church in spite of her misery, she decided that what she needed to see that night was an image of Jesus on the cross. That Jesus, she felt, agonizing alone on the cross, would understand her—he had also known the garbage heap of life, and she would not be alone!

What she actually met at church that night was not a cricified Jesus, but an empty cross—the sign of victory and resurrection. She wondered suspiciously if the clean and tidy cross might not also be a sign of how some Christians can hold so tightly to the promise of victory that they refuse to see the messiness of life, the pain of the cross—both Jesus' cross and the crosses all people from time to time bear, God's judgment on systems that crucify, and, by implication, God's call to believers to resist and transform those systems.

Finally, we might draw from examples of healing of brokenheartedness and the suffering it entails to envision an alternate understanding of Jesus' atoning work on the cross. In refusing to use his children for his own needs, Dan, we remember, felt the pain of unmet needs and the agony that the system had meant for those who had preceded and accompanied him. We might suggest that this model is appropriate for understanding the doctrine of the atonement. Jesus, born into a sinful and refusing world, refused to participate in the ongoing refusals. In this way, he took upon himself the sins of the world—paying the price for that cycle of sin and alienation ultimately with his own life.

Healing from brokenheartedness restores the brokenhearted to community. It is a process where we experience love, acceptance, and grief (for our brokenheartedness and for what we in our brokenheartedness have done to others), where we take responsibility for our own healing and for responding graciously to the woundedness of others, and where we learn that we are limited, that life is ambiguous, and that those we love can let us down. (And where we may begin to forgive ourselves—stop blaming ourselves —for not being able to make it any different.) Through it we also learn to let go to the mystery of life and are restored to spontaneity, to a desire to love and a willingness to be loved, to an acceptance of ourselves and our human condition, and to an ability to trust. Twelve-step recovery groups call this process learning to "let go and let God." It leads us to a few concluding comments in chapter 9.

---

[1] Walter Wink, "The Powers made us do it," in *The Christian Century* (Nov. 1, 1995) Vol. 112, No. 3, p. 1017f.

[2] Donald A. Gowan, "Salvation as Healing," in *Ex Auditu* (1989) Vol. 5, p.12.

[3] See Paul Fiddes' *Past Event and Present Salvation* (Louisville, Westminster/John Knox Press, 1989) for a fuller elaboration on the dual focus of salvation and for an argument about how Jesus' work can evoke transformation in the believer.

[4] This reference to Klienman's work is taken from "Crucial Observations Which Need to Be Extended: Commentary of 'Psychopathology, Sin and the *DSM*: Convergence and Divergence'" by John McDargh in *Journal of Psychology and Theology* (1994) Vol. 22, No. 4, pp. 286–288.

[5] This story happened twenty-five years ago. Since then we have discovered the risk of giving aspirin and probably would give another product instead.

[6] I realize that "total depravity" need not mean "wretchedness" but points to the inability to choose the good. However, persons may experience their depravity as "wretchedness." In the case of the dances of alienation, "wretchedness" may be the primary experience of the self (especially the hidden self), which might also reflect one's experience of never being (or choosing the) good.

[7] Donald Gowan in "Salvation as Healing" shows how confession of sin can develop as one struggles to make meaning of the pain and loneliness that accompany illness. His argument from the realm of physical pain remarkably parallels the development of the dances of alienation we have described in Part III. He says: "We may summarize what has been learned from the prophetic promises and the psalms of lament as follows: pain (including illness and every type of disability) produces a sense of loneliness, which can often be very intense. If severe enough and long-lasting enough the loneliness results in alienation, from one's community and from God. The effects of alienation from human companions are self-pity and a decreased sense of self-worth. A desire for vindication may also appear. Alienation from God is typically expressed in terms of distance or silence—feeling that God does not care; or in terms of anger—feeling that God is an enemy. But then that sense of weakness, worthlessness, uncleanness may become the means to justify God, as they lead to a confession of sin" (p. 9).

[8] The classical doctrine of original sin has addressed this problem of isolation by insisting that "all have sinned, and fall short of the glory of God." We need not, then, experience our sinfulness as cutting us off from other people. We are no different from others. We are not then given license to sin but can take comfort that our sinfulness does not set us apart from others and is an inevitable part of the human condition. This theological tactic is helpful to many people, as they can then feel free to confess their sinfulness, knowing that they are not alone in their confession. Knowing that their choices often will reflect more their own self-interest than the common good, they can still feel free to "sin boldly." However, for those whose disease is a woundedness created by a refusal that they believe they somehow deserved, the language of original sin—original depravity—often works to reinforce their sense of their own unworthiness.

[9] Although none of our examples suggested justice seeking as part of healing, it is reasonable to expect that some attention to justice may be part of the healing process. The perpetrators of rape, incest, and other systemic forms of violation may well be challenged to stop their behavior and/or seek forgiveness or otherwise make amends. This making of amends is a common expectation in twelve-step recovery programs and is central to the prophetic wisdom that justice is expected in God's coming realm.

[10] From "When I Think of the Cross" from the musical *Natural High: A Folk Musical About God's Son* composed by Ralph Carmichael and Kurt Kaiser, copyright 1970 by Lexicon Music, Inc.

[11] A christology from the perspective of the brokenhearted would be similar in many ways to the different christologies being developed from those caught in the "underside of history." See for instance the collection of christological essays in *Reconstructing the Christ Symbol*, ed. by Maryanne Stevens (New York: Paulist Press, 1993), especially articles by Jaquelyn Grant, Marina Herrera, and

Rita Nakashima Brock, and *Asian Faces of Jesus*, ed. by R.S. Sugirtharajah (Maryknoll, N.Y.: Orbis Books, 1993), especially articles by C.S. Song, and Byung Mu Ahn.

[12] Mrs. Davies' response to *Jesus Christ Superstar* is perhaps akin to that of the writer of second Isaiah, whose narrative of the Suffering Servant draws the conclusion that, whereas the community wanted to see the wounds of the Suffering Servant as something he deserved, they came to realize instead that his suffering was for (and because of) them.

[13] Delores Williams, *Sisters in the Wilderness* (Maryknoll, N.Y.: Orbis Press, 1993), especially pp. 161–170.

[14] See Valerie Saiving Goldstein, "The Human Situation: A Feminine View," in *Journal of Religion* 40 (April 1960), pp. 100–112; Judith Plaskow, *Sex, Sin and Grace: Women's Experience and the Theologies of Reinhold Niebuhr and Paul Tillich* (New York: University Press of America, 1980); Susan Nelson Dunfee, "The Sin of Hiding," in *Soundings* LXV, 3, Fall 1982: 316–327.

[15] Rita Nakashima Brock, "And a Little Child Shall Lead Us," in *Christianity, Patriarchy, and Abuse*, Joanne Carlson Brown and Carole R. Bohn, eds. (New York: The Pilgrim Press, 1989), pp. 42–61.

[16] Rita Nakashima Brock, "Losing Your Innocence but Not Your Hope," in *Reconstructing the Christ Symbol*, edited by Maryanne Stevens (New York: Paulist Press, 1993), pp. 30–53. See also Kathleen Sands, *Escape from Paradise* (Minneapolis: Fortress Press, 1994) for explication of the danger and elusiveness of innocence for human beings in an ambiguous and tragic world.

[17] See the Presbyterian Church (USA) Brief Statement of Faith where Jesus is confessed as one who proclaimed the reign of God by "healing the sick and binding up the brokenhearted" as well as "forgiving sinners."

[18] This phrase—admittedly a twentieth-century one—is borrowed from Robin Norwood's *Women Who Love Too Much: When You Keep Wishing and Hoping He'll Change* (New York: Pocket Books, 1985).

[19] It is, of course, tricky to talk about who Jesus really was, since what we have in the Gospels is the remembrance of the early community and not a picture free from that construction.

[20] In the Middle-Eastern culture this makes no sense. Surely, as Syrian Christians told me, he must have had cousins and aunts and uncles in Bethlehem. To be born so alone would be a sign of shame. (Thanks to Rev. Bchara Moussa Oghli for this insight.)

[21] This might be the insight of the *christus victor* view of the atonement—that Christ shared the captivity of those caught in cycles of sin. However, in this schema, Christ saves because he is innocent of sin (whereas everyone else is not); the forces of evil have captured the wrong man. In the schema of brokenheartedness, all victims (and not only Jesus) are initially innocent (except for their inadvertent participation in structures of sin pointed out in our discussion of inherited sin).

[22] See Paul Fiddes, *The Creative Suffering of God* (Oxford: Clarendon Press, 1988) for an argument that grounding God's suffering through the crucifixion to God's eternal trinitarian nature is also a way to strengthen the power of the image.

Chapter 9

Who Is the God in Whom We Trust?

Praise Me, says God;
I will know that you love Me.
Curse Me, says God;
I will know that you love Me.
Sing out My graces, says God.
Raise your fist against Me and revile.
Sing out My praises or revile.
Reviling is also a kind of praise, says God.
But if you sit fenced off
in your apathy, says God,
If you sit entrenched in:
"I don't give a hang,"
If you look at the stars and yawn,
If you see suffering and don't cry out,
If you don't praise and don't revile,
Then I created you in vain.

—Aaron Zeitlin[1]

For some of us, who not only suffer from brokenheartedness, but also have become conscious of it and seen it through to its source in historic acts of refusal, the question emerges: how could God have allowed such refusals to happen? How can we trust in—let go to—the mystery of life when life has broken us? Who is the God in whom we can trust? And what presuppositions about God undergird these questions?

Kay, as recounted in chapter 7, had a vision of a raging river and experienced in "letting go" something supporting her that at that time she called "love." This was not the end of Kay's story. In time she came to think of this "love" as God. And so she learned when life overwhelmed her to let go and trust God. When she felt overwhelmed, she would relax and conjure her river and reexperience her letting go. However, two years after her initial experience, Kay began to confront the early childhood experiences that had been echoed in her time of chaos. It was at this point that the idea of trusting God became problematic for her. "I know it works to let go of my worry and trust the flow of love that will support me," she said, "but I don't know why I should trust a God who let such awful things happen to me in the first place. If I 'let go and let God,' how can I know that God is any more reliable than God was in my youth? Who is the God in whom I put my trust?" For Kay, this was the beginning of a new exploration into the nature of her expectations of God. If God perhaps wasn't all powerful—if God didn't let awful things happen to her—then she could make some sense of her initial experiences of trauma. But how could she trust a God who didn't seem to rescue people from tragic situations? If the God who was in control and could do all that she wanted God to do (which would imply that saving her from her trauma was not God's inclination) was a God created in her youth to explain her sorrow (which she personally came to suspect), then who was the God in whom she now sought to trust?

Kay's dilemma is not unusual for victims of refusal and brokenheartedness. Just as trusted people in their lives seem to have let them down, so many survivors of many types of horror wonder if a God who "lets" these things happen is a God worth trusting at all. Many theologians—in response to these and similar issues—have sought to understand God in new ways. Pastoral theologian Nancy Ramsay, for example, argues that in the context of the shame of sexual abuse, it is better to think of God as a God who saves but who cannot keep us safe.[2]

A young girl lies in her bed at night listening to her parents fighting again—threatening one another with divorce. She hides her head under her pillow, knowing that her world is about to come to an end. In the midst of her fear, she prays over and over again to God, "Please, God, make them stop." But, as Betsy Petersen herself tells the story:

> ...they did not stop. Finally, I prayed, "Please God, make me stop crying." I felt something like a loving hand laid on my chest, firmly but not heavily. My breathing slowed, my tears stopped, and sleep shut out the rest of the quarrel.[3]

What kind of God is it who doesn't stop the fighting but quiets the frightened child; who doesn't stop the abuse but protects a child, perhaps through coping devices that blunt the full terror (coping devices that can themselves become the source of the dances of alienation we have explored)?

While the focus of this book has been on sin and brokenheartedness, we must also acknowledge these questions about God that emerge from our study and sketch out a vision of God that might correspond to a theology that takes seriously the condition of brokenheartedness. Theologian Wendy Farley, in *Tragic Vision and Divine Compassion*, offers the most satisfying reply to this dilemma I have yet to find.[5] Who is God of this tragic world? she asks. And in the light of brokenheartedness and sin[6] she answers: God is love; God is compassion. This love, she argues, is evident in three ways.

First, God is creative love. God in love creates a world that is not God—thus it is finite; it is free; it is diverse. This means that complexity, ambiguity, conflict, death, and the possibility for brokenheartedness and sin are built into creation itself. In this sense, God is the ground of brokenheartedness; in risking a free and finite creation (as well as creating creatures that are vulnerable and capable of great caring), God takes the risk that we might use our freedom to refuse others as well as to love them.

Second, God is sustaining love. To this wonderfully free, ambiguous, complex, and often tragic and sinful world, God is present as compassionate love that suffers with the world and loves it through its suffering. If brokenheartedness isolates us so we suffer alone, God's sustaining love will not let us go.

Third, God is redeeming love. God sustains this creation in its suffering; but God also expresses God's love as outrage at our wickedness toward one another. God's redeeming love is a love that remembers us in our brokenness and is the ground for our consciousness (whereby we see both our brokenheartedness and our sin) and for resistance to our human propensity to replicate cycles of refusal. This means that despite a world where it often appears that sin and refusals that result in brokenheartedness have the upper hand—where cycles of brokenheartedness repeat themselves, where refusals are institutionalized in racist, sexist, classist systems—there is another world order of love that grounds healing, justice, mercy, the mystery of life that sustains the world and will not be overcome. This redeeming love of God does not always "win" by the standards of a brokenhearted world. Sometimes those who love end up on crosses. But it is a love that will not be overcome.[7]

One Sunday morning in November, I find myself sitting in a small interracial congregation on the edge of the hill district in Pittsburgh singing the refrain:

> Jesus is the answer,
>   for the world today.
> Above him there's no other,
>   Jesus is the way.

It is a song that echoes back to my past. When I sang it then, it meant to me that Jesus was the only way to God, the only way to heaven. No other religious tradition—no other answer was adequate.

But on this particular morning, I have just come to the conclusion of this book, and I am aware of the brokenheartedness that fills this room and our surrounding neighborhoods. In our city in the past few weeks, a black man has been killed while being arrested by police. Whether a judge finally rules that Johnny Gammage's death was the result of police brutality or the tragic result of acceptable police efforts to restrain him, his death has been the context in which other stories have been told of racism and of police misuse of authority and force. People in this congregation bear the wounds of such refusals. There are other vestiges of brokenheartedness as well. Our city is no different from others. Women are raped and beaten, children are abused, hopeful parents from around the world bring their sick children to our hospitals for what—in their hometowns—would be miracle healings (and other children are brought to these hospitals by the very parents who have beaten them); people suffer from alcoholism; families split apart and kids are left to wonder what will happen to them; adults bear the wounds of childhoods where parents were unable, for whatever reason, to give them the love and nurture they needed.

In the context of this brokenheartedness, I hear the words to this song in a new way. In a world that breaks people's hearts, these people are singing that sin and brokenheartedness are not the final word. That the love of God—a word spoken to the world in the life of Jesus—is the highest, the final word—a word that cannot be overcome. That love is the source of our healing, the ground of mystery that is life. It is also the root of our survival and hope—a hope that works with the love of God to bring that word to fruition. As Hallie, one of the main characters in Barbara Kingsolver's novel *Animal Dreams*, counsels her sister:

> Codi, here's what I've decided: the very least you can do in your life is to figure out what you hope for. And the most you can do is live inside that hope. Not admire it from a distance but live right in it, under its roof. What I want is so simple I almost can't say it: elementary kindness. Enough to eat, enough to go around. The possibility that kids might one day grow up to be

neither the destroyers nor the destroyed. That's about it. Right now I'm living in that hope, running down its hallway and touching the walls on both sides.[8]

---

[1] Thanks to Candace Veon for this poem.

[2] See Nancy J. Ramsay's article, "Sexual Abuse and Shame: the Travail of Recovery," in *Women in Travail and Transition*, Maxine Glaz and Jeanne Stevenson Moessner, eds. (Minneapolis: Fortress Press, 1991), pp. 109–125. Process theologians also argue for a God who is not all-powerful in the sense of coercive power. They picture God's power as the power of persuasion—leaving open the possibility that creation can reject God's persuasive power.

[3] Betsy Petersen, *Dancing with Daddy: A Childhood Lost and a Life Regained* (New York: Bantam Books, 1991), p. 137.

[4] Another approach to understanding who God is in the midst of brokenheartedness is demonstrated by Robin Crawford. Working with recovering alcoholics and helping them to image God in a new way, he asks them to remember times in their lives when they felt most sane. This then has led to new insights into how God works in people's lives. See "Trouble in the Family of God: The Effects of Household Chaos on Relations with God," in *Church and Society*, May/June 1992, pp. 25–34.

[5] Wendy Farley is not the only theologian who has wrestled with how we understand God in the face of evil and radical suffering. Her answer, that God is with us in the midst of suffering, is one that other theologians have explored as well. For a recent review of much of this literature and for an argument for the suffering of God, see Paul Fiddes, *The Creative Suffering of God* (Oxford: Oxford University Press, 1988). Fiddes misses, however, the work of feminist and womanist theologians from North America.

[6] Farley's term for innocent suffering that deeply wounds the soul of the sufferer is "radical suffering." This term is not identical to my terms of brokenheartedness or refusal, for she means by radical suffering something more life-threatening than I necessarily mean by refusal. However, her category points to undeserved suffering and raises the question of how we understand God in the face of such suffering.

[7] See Delores Williams, *Sisters in the Wilderness*, for an argument against those who too easily would name God the God of liberation. The oppressed, she notes, are not always set free; often all they do is survive. God, she says, the God of Hagar, rather, is a God who "makes a way out of no way," who is the ground of survival and hope.

[8] Barbara Kingsolver, *Animal Dreams* (New York: Harper-Collins Publishers, 1990), p. 299.